The *

Duck Tape

Devotional

*40 Day

The *
Duck Tape
Devotional

*

40 Day

Karen Lemon

ISBN: 9781798567821
Imprint: Independently published

Dedication

For The Special "J's" in my life

Jesus

Julia

Jean

Joyce

John

But, my son, be warned:
there is no end of opinions
ready to be expressed.
Studying them can go on forever
and become very exhausting!

Ecclesiastes 12:12
Living Bible (TLB)

Forward

"Duck" Tape Devotional??? Isn't the proper term "Duct" Tape? Yes, I do know the difference but calling a devotional Duct Tape may sound like it's something for spiritual HVAC workers; which would really limit the readership. No offense to those in the heating and air conditioning industry. I mean, who doesn't like ducks??? I suppose if you've been attacked by one there might be some animosity regarding the little feather-ball, but hopefully it can be overcome. I mean I've met more benevolent ducks than mean ones. Although the one that bit my ankle because I wouldn't share my funnel cake was more of a food motivated attack. Somehow, I just couldn't blame the little guy for trying. Although, as a nurse, I also didn't want to be responsible for contributing to the unhealthy lifestyle of a diabetic duck.

The other reason for the title is that duct tape is so versatile. It's been used for everything from the original usage to all those little fix-it jobs that need something flexible and strong, even though I think putting a car bumper back on with it is a little over the top. But, hey, I've seen it done and it appears to work. Not attractive at all, but very practical.

Which reminds me of ducks. The little guys are so versatile… they fly, they swim, and they walk on land. It's just like the Marines, but with feathers. And ducks are all over the place. You go to the lake and what do you find? Ducks. You go to the park and what do you find? Ducks. You try to eat a funnel cake and what attacks you? Your kids. But if your kids aren't there then most likely a duck will find you. Ducks are everyday critters. Duct tape is an everyday fix-it solution. If you have duck tape, well you have the best of everyday life.

And isn't that what most of our life is about? Everyday situations make up the majority of life and most of us overlook it or don't appreciate it. How about everyday life and spirituality??? I'm sure we would all like to have exciting, mountaintop God experiences every day; but, that's not how life seems to work. How does our beliefs intersect with everyday living? That's what this book is about.

This book is not going to give you the secret steps to living an incredibly successful life, claiming wealth and winning and being a happy clam all the time. I've read those books, I've tried those ideas and the only conclusion I could come to is that I failed at being able to do all that was prescribed. But I have waddled on past all of those books and came to my own conclusion. My beliefs and everyday life have merged in an interesting way and perhaps you can see a similar pattern in your own life. The following devotional is nothing more than everyday stories and situations that have come along in my life and I discovered a connection. There will be no steps to follow and no instant solutions... just everyday ducks trying to find spiritual tape to help with situations in our everyday lives.

Come and waddle along.

How to use this book

Each day has a different devotional subject and can be read daily if desired. Some of these subjects involve holidays, special events, historical information, etc. To help organize these better I have made a listing of "themes" that have to do with that particular day's devotional. If it is around Christmas and you want to find the specific readings for that holiday, they are listed below. If you get stopped by the police regarding speeding, you can go directly to that subject. Ever wonder how Gettysburg and spiritual warfare are connected? Yuppers, that's in there also.

I think you will find the below directory quite helpful if you are a more A type personality. All B types feel free to just dive right in! Above all… enjoy!

Holidays
Valentine's Day	Days	28, 36
Thanksgiving	Day:	20
Christmas	Days:	1, 14, 16, 37

Leisure
Sports and Games	Days:	11, 34, 35, 40

Special Times
Gift-giving	Days:	1, 7
Surprise	Days:	2, 5, 24

Who are you and where are you going?
Identity	Days:	4, 9, 13, 22, 23, 25, 30, 35
Direction	Days:	6, 26, 29
Perspective	Days:	17, 21, 33, 38

Oh dear…
Storms	Days:	3, 5, 19

Speeding   Day: 39
Security   Days: 10, 15

Answers? What Answers?
Duh – I don't know   Days: 8, 12, 32

It's good to know
Lessons and Love   Days: 18, 27, 31

Table of Contents

Day 1

God's Presence In Presents

Remember the line from this popular musical: "Brown paper packages tied up with string, these are a few of my favorite things?" If you have never agreed with this particular theory of package covering choices (after all, brown is not the most attractive wrapping for a present nor a Hallmark bestseller), you may change your mind by the end of this.

One of my recurrent (otherwise known as a broken record player) prayers is thanking God for the "gift of one another." I never want to take for granted all the wonderful gifts or presents that have been given to me by God in the form of those persons around me. So, I started making the analogy of people being presents. Let me first explain that all presents have two parts: the "outer" wrapping and the "inner" contents (see... my many years of education did pay off after all to share that kind of sound reasoning and logic!).

Now, the wrapping can come in any and all types with the sizes and shapes being equally dramatic and varied. From the classic Victorian designs, to pretty pastels, to bold abstracts, to one solid color, to... well, frankly, the possibilities are endless. Along the way, I have run into a few that have been; oh, let's call them, "unique." As examples, there have been the few decorated with flashing lights, some with spiked bows and pierced ribbons; a few have had complex philosophical theories scrawled over them; some the paper was haphazardly placed about it; an occasional one is torn in places, sometimes repaired, sometimes still ripped; one even looked like it fell off the UPS truck and was run over, the tire tracks still imprinted upon it. The ones in the Army were all OD (for you non-military types that stands for olive drab green, the fashion statement color of the armed forces). In addition, a few have been very difficult to open, and on the rare occasion, one or two have NEVER been opened. I found some that were wrapped over and over in heavy packaging tape which took a long time to unravel (hurriedly cutting it open seemed to me to be a bad idea); another was intertwined with lots of string and knots but with patience it could be untied; and then there were a couple encased in metal or put in a lock box with no indication of where the key could be located. But for those that could be entered the contents were as equally intriguing as the outside wrappings.

First, there was the very large package that only had one or two small items inside. On the other hand, a little tiny package burst open and spilled out more than it looked like it could possibly have held. Some of the contents were a real mystery as to what they even were, and on occasion the owner of the package didn't have an explanation about them either. A few let you look at the contents but not touch them. Some allowed you to touch the contents, but they had to be returned. And then there were a couple who gave away the contents as they thought best; yet, they always seemed to have more, even when you thought they had given away the last one. Always you could find a package that was EMPTY. When I was younger, I used to be disappointed by this, that there was nothing there for me, but now it is an opportunity to place something of mine in the package, especially when no one is watching, making it a welcome surprise!

But the most important trait, no matter what the trappings are inside or out: ALL the packages that knew God in a personal way were found to have a light inside - always illuminating the box inwardly… no matter what other contents were there, and sometimes even when it was empty.

NOW, I have a "double-dog dare" for all of you!!! Sit down with paper and lots of colored markers and draw the present that you are as you view yourself. Then write out what you would find inside.   And, oh… by the way… how's the lighting in there?

"I revealed myself to those who did not ask for me;
I was found by those who did not seek me."
- Isaiah 65:1

Day 2

Mr. Clean And The Unexpected Gems Of Life

Well… it was better than Belgium candy. That was my thought as an unexpected gift was given in thanks for helping a family friend with some chores around her home. As a child, I was given chores to do. I did chores around the house and yard, AND my mother would send me to help with chores of neighbors and friends in need. There was no payment for my helping, it was just the right thing to do, and it was mother's direction to do so as well. This was one of those neighborhood helping chores that came my way when I was growing up.

There was a friend of our family who lived nearby, an elderly woman who immigrated to the United States from Belgium, and although she was not a relative, we called her Aunt Helen. She was a rather large woman who hugged and kissed you every time she saw you, and I harbored a fear of being smothered, even being a junior high student, since she had quite a bear hug that was all encompassing. Now, after providing help to Aunt Helen, there was a gift given on each occasion and it came in the form of your choice of a piece of Belgium candy. There was always a large dish of it in her dining room and she would insist that you take a piece after assisting her. The candy was the hard kind that you had to dissolve in your mouth for a long period of time, so the taste would be with you for what seemed to be an eternity. With Belgium candy… this is not a good thing. Let me explain that Belgium candy is unique, or at least Aunt Helen's was, in that it had the flavor of… well, the only thing I can compare it with is… perfume. The closest I have come to eating anything similar is "rose flavored" Turkish Delight, a candy

3

produced in Britain. You may recall that Edmund, in <u>The Lion, The Witch, and The Wardrobe,</u> is asked by the White Witch what would he most desire in all the world, and his answer was... Turkish Delight. What Edmund was thinking is beyond me, but I think perhaps he needed to get out more often. The boy should have been introduced to Dove chocolates at the very least. But... I digress.

This day, however, was different at Aunt Helen's because she had dropped within my hand two rings. They were of costume jewelry quality, but for a young girl in junior high school, each was a treasure. One had four sparkling stones of clear crystal, two teardrop and two rectangular in shape. Once in the sunlight when I was departing Aunt Helen's home, the ring was blinding. To me, it was beyond beautiful. The other ring, however, had one stone which was of medium size and of rectangular shape. It was gray in color and looked very old and worn. It did not sparkle in the least, even in the bright summer sunshine, and I hardly gave it a second notice since the other ring had already become my favorite.

About a week or so later, my mother decreed that my chore for the day was to wash the baseboards and exposed wooden floors in the living and dining room. This was not an easy task since it requires being on your hands and knees, using a bucket and rag, rinsing often, and wiping each corner and edging. It is time consuming and, in the process, I got to know Mr. Clean very well during this undertaking. Now, I liked my clear crystal ring so much I had not taken it off since receiving it, but, knowing that my hands would be in "wash water" I did not want my precious gift to be exposed to such a strong detergent (after all, it's not called Mr. Clean for nothing!). I looked at the "other" ring in its gray dullness and decided that if anything deserved to be in the wash water, this item was it. I placed that undesirable ring on my finger, not concerned if it was ruined, and went about completing the chore. I paid no mind to the ring at all while I was cleaning, since my attention was upon being thorough and scrubbing each part of the baseboard and flooring perfectly. If I did not, I would be doing it over, and that option did not appeal to me. I went into the basement to dispose of the dirty wash water and I gasped in looking at my hand. The ring was now a sparkling turquoise blue crystal and was even more beautiful than the clear crystal ring I had come to favor!!!

What amazing surprises we can discover in our lives in doing such everyday chores and allowing a cleansing of God to come in such unexpected ways. May you also find a sparkling gem of life in the same way today.

"The kingdom of heaven is like treasure hidden in a field."

4

- Matthew 13:44

Day 3

The "Not So Secret" Storm

For being midmorning, I noticed that the forest was growing dark… very, very dark. Clouds were increasing and becoming more ominous as I hiked further on. At that point, I was debating if I should turn back and head to the Army base I was stationed at in Germany. But I was already almost two hours away and I would not be able to return before this storm broke forth. The first flash of lightning was so brilliant that it took me by surprise, and I was visibly startled before standing still. The clap of thunder followed loudly. It was not a comforting feeling.

I remember thinking… now what do I do? I am in the middle of a very thick forest, on a small pathway, surrounded by an endless array of tall trees… not the best place to be during an electric storm. I decided to turn around and head back to my base, but as I did, the rain came, slowly at first, but increasing to a driving deluge in a very short period of time. I could feel the wetness slowly soaking through my clothes, but I was grateful that at least it was a warm rain. Wearing glasses in such a situation does not help matters either, since the lenses easily took on the drops of water and I could not see very well down the pathway. Taking them off was not much better, since I am just slightly above being blind without them.

With each step, the storm seemingly increased in intensity. I recall the lightning at times being blinding, even as the thunder was deafening, and it became more consistent. I wondered what it would feel like to be struck by lightning, but even in my best imaginings, I could only think that it would hurt… a lot! I had been

6

talking to God just as a matter of prayer and conversation well before the storm was even beginning, but now I had become very practical in thinking what I "should" do regarding the storm. The solution was simple... there was nothing I could do. I could not leave the forest and the storm was not stopping. I was feeling rather helpless, to say the least.

About that time, I noticed a group of pine trees nearby which were very tightly grouped together. In fact, they were so tightly packed that their branches intertwined between each other and the pine needles underneath were actually dry. I came closer and noted that I could crawl under the outlying branches and within was a hiding place that was quite cozy. The practical part of me said that hiding under a tree during an electric storm was not safe, but then, wasn't I in a forest where there were only trees? Did it really make any difference which trees I was taking shelter under? It was an interesting situation with very few options, so I made myself comfortable and settled into my hiding place.

I suddenly became aware of how softly the rain was falling upon the forest in whispering sounds. The lightning came in patterns of light through the tightly crossing branches, and the thunder seemed quieter in this sheltered place. I felt safe and there was a peacefulness amid this very intense storm. God seemed very close indeed!

Recently I have been struggling with some issues in my life that have been difficult, and, at times, it has felt as though I have been surrounded by incessant storms. The other night I was recalling my time in the forest during this storm and realized that it was very symbolic of what I am going through at the present time. In the same way, God has graciously provided a place that is peaceful and safe in Him from these present storms of life. All I need to do is to go there.

In the midst of the storms in your life... may you do so as well.

**"Now may the God of peace Himself sanctify you entirely;
and may your spirit and soul and body be preserved complete..."
- I Thessalonians 5:23**

Day 4

A Martha Or Mary Lifestyle

So, you say you don't know of Martha? The Martha from the village of Bethany! Oy vey! You must be hanging out in the pig troughs with the prodigal son not to know of Martha. Remember the last Bar Mitzvah? Who could forget such an event with all the gefilte fish, matzo ball soup, lox, bagels, latkes… my mouth drools just thinking about the food she served. And the presentation! How Martha ever made all those plates, one for each of the 12 tribes of Israel, with the actual clay from each location, as well as taking the time to mold each one into the symbol for each tribe. Well, it's beyond me! The table even… did you know and are you sitting down, Martha imported the wood from the cedars of Lebanon? Sure, it took such a long time, but people are still talking about it! Let me tell you, you can't even buy a reputation like that!!!

So, you say you know of Mary. Hmmm, no, she's not at all like her sister. Mary doesn't know a gefilte fish from a matzo ball, that I can tell you. She spends too much time listening. No, not to gossip but to teachings. Did you hear how interested she is in that rabbi who's been teaching so much around town. So many people following him everywhere, like a bunch of sheep. He even calls Himself – the Good Shepherd! I can tell you that the religious leaders do not agree with Him at all. Mary better be careful also and it's about time she gets interested in what her sister Martha is doing. Martha is a fine young woman.

8

Now here's the latest story about these two. This rabbi, Yeshua, comes to visit Martha and Mary at their home! Can you believe it? As usual, Martha holds back nothing in the preparations for Him. I mean when He arrives she is still working at all the eloquent details: the meats which she raised from handfed kosher calves; the salads and vegetables grown in the hothouse during the winter months then transplanted to the fields; the desserts with fresh raisins and almonds brought back from Nazareth just a few days before; digging the clay to create the pottery for the dishes and cups, weaving the tablecloth after gathering the wool from the sheep, the same ones that she raised from lambs; and I could go on and on. But then there's Mary just sitting and listening to Rabbi Yeshua talking and teaching while her poor sister works herself into the ground. And so, Martha asks Him, "Lord, don't you care that my sister has left me to do the work by myself? Tell her to help me?" "Martha, Martha," the Lord answered, "you are worried and upset about many things, but only one thing is needed. Mary has chosen what is better and it will not be taken away from her." (Luke 10:38-42)

Can you believe such a thing? WHAT IS HE THINKING?????

"There is a time for everything, and a season for every activity under heaven."
- Ecclesiastes 3:1

Day 5

The Mess That Became Blessed

It was a messy vacation. And, as you know, vacations SHOULD not be messy. Vacations SHOULD be all that is good and right in the world. Vacations SHOULD be the perfect time away from the breakneck, hectic, insane lives that we live. Vacations SHOULD be a time of enjoying everything that is offered: the sun, the fun, the activities, the nice weather, the...

Indeed, I had all those countless preconceived ideas and plans for this time away at the beach. Yes, this SHOULD be everything... except ... messy.

Who would have thought that a hurricane in the Gulf of Mexico heading for Louisiana would have had any effect on a beach in, of all places, South Carolina? I've looked at the maps and the two are not even close!!! But Isidore, (is it me, or was anyone else confused on whether that was a guy or gal's name?) spread waaaaay out to the east, curled around Florida, and sent bands of itself to... MY VACATION!!!

So, I formed my plan on how to outsmart this hurricane. I watched the weather channel and saw the break between those bands of rain showers and then timed getting on my bicycle and riding like "stink" (translation: lightning fast) to the beach. And so, I took a long walk, wading through the surf and watching those fantastic 6-foot waves. Now normally there are basically no waves on the beach, so they were only that high because of... that pesky hurricane. Imagine all that powerful beauty due to such a vacation wrecker. Hmmmmm.

Leaving the beach, I decided to see more of the island and while on my biking adventure... suddenly one of those Doppler radar rainstorm bands came right over me and poured. Within record moments I was soaked completely, watching the bike path through the powerful waterfall running off my bike helmet directly in front of my face. I felt I was reliving my time on the Maid of the Mist at the base of Niagara Falls. With the poor visibility of peering through the rain (and helmet water shed) I missed the signs showing how to return to where I was staying. And so, I kept riding and riding... and it kept raining and raining... and suddenly when it seemed like I would be doing this forever... I started laughing. The humor of the moment overtook me, and with it I began noticing the wonder about me as well as within me. I noted that everything was so green and smelled so fresh...including me. The moment rivaled an Irish Spring commercial. Laughing was freeing and shortly after that I saw the condo at which I was staying.

There is something about being totally soaking wet and entering an air-conditioned room. Ice formed on my clothes... ok, well, not really, but it felt like it. It is amazing how quickly you can draw a warm bath and jump in. I am thinking about lobbying for it to be an Olympic event because I know I would win the gold easily! I changed into dry clothes, put on my poncho (for the record, it is Army issue camouflage) and walked to a most wonderful restaurant. Sitting by the window, looking at the harbor, having a great dinner, watching the rain and wind and waves... I felt so warm, cozy, and contented. I could picture Jesus across from me smiling at my absolute surprise at what a blessing this had all become.

There was a comfort around me that I had not felt in years. Perhaps it is because I never walk in the rain and get soaked any more. Perhaps it is because I have so many preconceived ideas of how life SHOULD be. Perhaps God can reach into our lives with blessings that totally take us by surprise. Perhaps it is time to stop SHOULDING in our lives.

"But I will send you the Comforter – the Holy Spirit, the source of all truth.
He will come to you from the Father and will tell you all about me."
- John 15:26

Day 6

Blah, Blah, Blah…

It seems that I find myself talking so much over the course of the day… and, of course, realize that all of us are doing the same! In filtering through this endless stream of ideas expressed, I thought it would be interesting to bring just a few to your attention. Hopefully, this will provide some solace, wisdom, and entertainment to our otherwise demanding lives. Enjoy!!!!!

"Over the years, the United States has sent many of its fine young men and women into great peril to fight for freedom beyond our borders. The only amount of land we have ever asked for in return is enough to bury those that did not return." Colin Powell

"I know God won't give me anything I can't handle. I just wish he didn't trust me so much." Mother Teresa

"Don't come running to me when you break your leg." Everyone's Mother

"You don't manage people, you manage things. You lead people." Grace Murray Hopper, Admiral, U.S. Navy, Retired

"God! The way you treat your friends, no wonder you have so few."

(While helping to push a carriage caught in a flash flood in waist deep water and mud.) St. Teresa of Avila

"Be your own entertainment center."   Loretta LaRoche, Speaker on Stress Management

"The need is not the call." Norma Scott, Bobby Scott's Mother

"We know what we are, but know not what we become." William Shakespeare

"Failure to plan is to plan to fail." Bill Phillips, Founder of Body For Life

"More is not always better." A poster above the desk of Major Francis Mara, Chaplain, U.S. Army

"Paula, Iraq has made a grave tactical error. When they launched a scud missile at this camp, they clearly hoped to deter the Marines. Instead, Paula, they've made them very, very angry." CNN correspondent embedded with the Marines reporting back to Paula Zahn

"You take your job seriously, but not yourself. Have fun."   The motto for employees at Chili's Restaurants

"When you bury feelings, you bury them alive." Toni Mills Clayton, Counselor

"Each heart knows its own bitterness, and no one else can share its joy." Proverbs 14:10

"Pay attention and listen to the sayings of the wise;
apply your heart to what I teach,
for it is pleasing when you keep them in your heart
and have all of them ready on your lips."
- Proverbs 22:17-18

Day 7

Building Up – A Personal Perspective About Life

There once was a couple who had two children. These parents had concerns about their two young sons, because each child was the very opposite of the other. The one was the most extreme pessimist they had ever seen, and, in contrast, the other was the eternal optimist. As with all parents who want to do the right thing in raising children, it was discussed that since the twin's birthday was approaching, they would use this event to modify their children's perspectives. Honestly, they didn't discuss it that calmly or philosophically as you can imagine. If you just think of the last time you talked about some important issue regarding your children's behavior… well, need I say more? The couple; however, did come up with an agreeable plan to address their concerns.

Starting months before the twin's birthday the parents agreed to listen to ALL the items that the pessimist said he wanted for his birthday and purchase them. They reasoned that it would be impossible for this child to be pessimistic because he would have received everything he wanted. On the other hand, the only thing they would give the optimist was, well, a room filled with horse "pucky" (translation = manure). Surely this child could not find one positive comment about a room full of… well, you know what.

The months went by and the birthday arrived with each of the children running to see what presents he had received. The pessimist entered the room and every present had his name on it, so he hurriedly opened each one. After he was finished the parents asked, "Well, what do you think?" Sighing, he whined, "I got a ball,

14

but it's the wrong color. And I got a bike, but it's raining outside. Each present was greeted with a similar negative reply. The parents, of course, were disappointed. In reality, that's an understatement, but you get the point.

The optimist watched this whole scenario excitedly and then asked, "What did I get for my birthday?" The parents pointed to the door to the "ROOM." In an attempt to be tactful, I'm trying not to use the "pucky" word too much. With great anticipation the little boy opened the door, entered and closed the door behind him. A great deal of time went by and the parents were beginning to worry that perhaps this measure had been too extreme. Surely, he would be out shortly in tears realizing that there was nothing positive about this "present." Just as expected the door flung open and the boy came out shaking and shouting. "Ohhhhhh! Ohhhhhhhhh! I got a horse!!!! But he ran away!!!!!!!!!!!!!!

Now think about how you would react to a room full of everything you ever wanted. Duh? Like that's going to happen in this lifetime!!! Or if you received a room full of horse pucky. Been there, done that already perhaps?

In any case, I have some great ideas for birthday presents if you need them. Oh, I almost forgot, please let me know if you've seen my horse wandering about!

"For the Lord gives wisdom, and from his mouth comes knowledge and understanding."
- Proverbs 2:6

Day 8

A Personal History Of "I Don't Know"

Do you realize how often we use phrases for reasons other than what they truly mean? "I don't know" has always been a personal favorite of mine. I first encountered this phrase when I was little, I mean really little. Back then "I don't know" meant... well, at that point it really did mean what it said. Let's face it, I had a lot to learn and with this phrase I was given a wealth of knowledge. Some of it I found out later was not quite accurate and included made up answers. Can you imagine that? It was then I realized that grown-ups don't usually say "I don't know." Rather what they mean is: You think I really do know everything, or perhaps I'm supposed to, and I'd like to keep it that way. In other words, what would you really think if I admitted I didn't know everything? But I'm getting ahead of myself for now. Let me digress for the moment

When I was in elementary school "I don't know" really indicated that I was most likely day-dreaming. An example I recall is: "Which planet in our solar system might be able to sustain life? I heard a question somewhere in my day-dream, however, not enough to answer. So, do I make up an answer (which seemed like the grown-up thing to do) or do I say: "I don't know." Well, I took the risk and gave the most incorrect answer this side of the galaxy, to the laughter of the entire class and with the teacher trying to keep a straight face. I learned a very valuable lesson – unless you're a grown-up don't try to make up an answer. Grown-ups have much more experience than your limited life time and your chances of success are basically zero.

Then came high school, and another meaning of that familiar phrase developed. It was during a softball game and I was on third base. Our team was behind by one run with two outs in the bottom of the ninth inning. This was it, I could tie the score and so I tried to steal home plate on a wild pitch. Nice idea, but the catcher threw herself right in my path to slide. As I recall she was a very large individual (most catchers are) and I was not. It was like a VW bug hitting a semi at 60 mph. After I was scraped off the field my coach asked why I had done that. What came out of my mouth was "I don't know." It was not one of my more impressive moments.

As my late teens rolled around, I decided to join the Army… you know, Army Strong, An Army of One, Be All You Can Be, Join The People Who've Joined the Army, etc. To say the least, "I don't know" was not a popular phrase, and I did many extra push-ups, sit-ups, and running to remove it from my vocabulary. I did become "all I could be" and, in addition, I don't recall ever saying "I don't know" for the remainder of my enlistment.

Next academia became a part of my life with college and nursing school. I studied and was prepared for those questions that professors like to ask. In nursing school "I don't know" was not acceptable, especially when asked a question in the operating room by a surgeon. Instead, I explained all that I did know on the subject, whether it answered the question or not. I realized then that if I didn't make it as an RN, I could always go into politics.

Now that I've been an adult for a while, I've seen some other questions arise in my life and others. Sometimes it's the tougher side of events that come our way – tragic events, the death of a loved one, illnesses, emotional challenges, etc. So often I hear the questions relating to these events and I have attempted to come up with the answer for a countless number of reasons. My answers have been so inadequate that it finally occurred to me that maybe there are some unknown mysteries in life and that I am OK without thinking I know everything… much less expressing it. I believe I've come full circle to rediscover the original meaning of the phrase "I don't know." Perhaps that's part of becoming "as a little child."

"And He said: "Truly I tell you, unless you change and become
like little children, you will never enter the kingdom of heaven."
- Matthew 18:3

Day 9

Who Do People Say YOU Are?

You are the sunshine of my life! You're crazy! You're a bloomin' wonder! You're one fry short of a Happy Meal! You're the berries! You're too much! You're one brick shy of a full load! You're the best thing since sliced bread! You're _____; please take a moment to fill in the blank. I have had a litany of these expressions used by various people throughout my life, and I will go out on a limb here and bet all of you have as well. Very few were solicited by me, while most were given without my asking or my interest. Some were flattering, some encouraging, some confusing, some insulting; but all of them were enlightening in one way or another.

About a week ago I was working with some volunteers who were helping with a project for the school. We were in the elementary teacher workroom and the statement was made, "Wow, that picture reminds me of you." In that room, there is only one picture, which stretches from ceiling to floor, advertising the Rockwell Exhibit when it was displayed at the High Museum in Atlanta. Who is on that huge poster? Well, let me stop for a moment and ask you personally, who would be on that poster if someone would associate it with you? Now, let's get more personal... who would you WANT to be on the poster that would be associated with you? How many of us would have the same answer to each, I wonder?

I have looked at this picture many, many times before; but now that another person was connecting me to it in an intimate way, the whole concept of "Who do people say I am?" met "Who do I think I am?" The process itself was an epiphany. I began to think about whom I would WANT to be on that poster and all sorts of imaginative, unrealistic, wishing sort of individuals came to mind, especially thin, attractive ones. The phrase that followed, echoing in my mind, was; "Oh sure... right... who are you kidding? Get real!" And so, realism comes like a bucket of cold water, waking one from those dream-like moments. I was forced to look at the figure in the painting once again, and this time I really saw her for who she was; and yes, the individual who made the original comment was on the mark… I have much in common with Rosie the Riveter.

Picture this… a large production line during World War II. It's lunchtime, and there sits a woman eating her sandwich, not a low-calorie salad, mind you, but a hearty, meaty type of sandwich. A sturdy, large framed gal with the tools of her new wartime trade setting on her lap, while her shoes use Hitler's manifesto, Mein Kampf, as a footrest. Goggles and safety shield pushed up, resting upon her bright red hair, while gritty overalls with rolled up shirt sleeves display rather massive biceps and arms. She has been working very hard with grease and dirt over her face, arms and hands; most likely she is sweaty as well. Many of us a few months ago would not have thought much of this individual, nor given her a second glance if she were transported "as is" to our present society where outward appearance, especially for women, is a priority. However, times change, and I think most of us would have heartily welcomed that "jump in and roll your sleeves up" kind of gal on September 11th in New York City or Washington D.C.

In the book of Mark, Jesus asks this very question of his disciples; "Who do people say I am?" Then He takes it to a more personal level by asking, "Who do you say I am?" I would challenge you this week to find someone you trust and ask them to answer that very same question. Listen with a hearing heart to the reply given, and then prayerfully seek out what you see inside yourself. What a great way to learn more of who we really are in our Lord Jesus and to grow in that knowledge.

"Jesus and his disciples went on to the villages around Caesarea Philippi. On the way He asked them, 'Who do people say I am?'"
- Mark 8:27

19

Day 10

For A Siren Song Of Peace

The sirens and the lights dimming made me wonder what was going on. I had to remind myself that I was in church on a Sunday morning as I looked upon the large screen at the front of the sanctuary and there was the image of the Twin Towers on 9-11 a number of years ago, once more, the scarred and torn footage forever etched in my mind. But this time it was the sound of the sirens in the background that seemed to make the impact, perhaps because we had been singing praise songs before that point and the change was as different as night and day.

Sirens have always been a call to action in the household I grew up in. Firefighters abound in our family, and when the local fire station's siren sounded it would be followed by dropping forks, running footsteps, and a yelping dog. I used to comment that I expected at some time to find our poor dog, Tiger, completely flattened on the carpet with a "waffled" boot print over him. The huge boots that came with a fireman's turnout gear were very awkward to run in, and Tiger had a habit in the excitement of the moment of getting in the way.

Please note that even if we were all sitting down to a holiday dinner, half of those at the table would get up and run out. My uncle was the fire chief in our town until he was forced to retire at age 65. My other uncle was a volunteer firefighter all his life and my brothers joined as soon as they were old enough to do so. My oldest brother is not only a volunteer but a professional firefighter as well. In my family we all listened for the siren to sound at any time, and so I had to almost slap myself to realize that I really was in church and hearing that familiar "call to arms." I had this urge to run... to help... someone... in some way....and the feeling of helplessness that I had a few years ago returned very powerfully.

Slowly the siren sounds were being replaced by a crescendo of music giving a message of hope. I looked down at that point and saw... an infant in the row in front of me. He (there was a blue blanket over the baby, so I will make the guess that it was a boy, even though that is probably politically, or "genderly," incorrect reasoning) was in one of those carriers with the top partially up to keep the light out of those big, beautiful eyes. Little hands were clinging to the blue blanket as legs kicked gently and he was all strapped in, so cozy and warm. The little smile over that face was so... peaceful. Gosh, the little guy looked so content and safe... and I... envied him. This baby had no idea about sirens, or terrorism, or planes, or such. This baby did not even know that he was helpless! At the same time the song that now overtook the entire congregation was one that echoed what this baby seemed to symbolize – "It Is Well With My Soul."

Even in those times in which we can do nothing to change the most tragic of circumstances, times we do not even understand our own helplessness, and perhaps even more when we do... Jesus can come and give such contentment and safety in the deepest parts of our being.

So, I suppose, the question remains, "How well is it with our souls?"

"Peace I leave with you; my peace I give you. I do not give as the world gives. Do not let your hearts be troubled and do not be afraid."
- John 14:27

Day 11

The Proverbial "Spiritual" Fastball

As a child, I had tons of energy. Endless abounding energy that took me from sun up, through the evening, and into the night… well, at least as late as my bedtime would allow. I lived in a neighborhood that had two excellent resources: it was a dead-end street which allowed us to play in the road with relative safety; and, most of the families on our block had kids, so there was an endless supply of teammates to play sports. I love sports! I always have and, if I do say so myself, was a rather decent athlete from a very early age. This love of sports was brought about because my brothers always needed another player, especially for baseball, and I was recruited as soon as I was able to stand and walk. Being recruited early in life for sports allows one to become very skilled in those endeavors. I stress this because you need to understand that an entire day of sports with lots of other kids was my idea of heaven at the time.

In our neighborhood, it was not unusual for all of us to play football, baseball, four-square, "in the soup", red-rover, kickball, and badminton, or any combination of those, all day long. All our youthful energy had to be used up, or at least our mothers certainly believed so. (As I write this I wonder about where that energy goes since science tells us that energy can be neither created nor destroyed. Obviously, mine has found better places to be nowadays, but I digress…). During these wonderful days of activity, I learned that darkness was an invader that came to spoil my day. It brought an ending to what I greatly enjoyed.

22

I recall, so very well, the evenings of playing baseball in particular. The sun would be going down and darkness would come… so… very… slowly. It softly fell as a dark velvet cloak coming to drape over the street, the bases, the players, and eventually the ball. We all knew it was getting dark, but no one wanted to admit it. I suppose back then we did not know to term it "denial," although the effect was still the same, no matter what it is titled. In our "denial" we would keep playing until everyone was striking out, even me (grin). You would think we would have a clue at that point but, we next would argue over whether the pitch was a ball or a strike. Mind you that no one could honestly even SEE the ball, but we KNEW that we were RIGHT. Reality, however, does eventually intervene and inevitably someone would get a pitch right into the cranium and with a howling scream of pain, one participant would FINALLY admit the obvious. "I think we better quit now, it's too dark to continue." I believe that kid grew up to be a successful counselor since he was able to help the rest of us come out of "darkness denial."

But, oh, how often I am in denial of the darkness that comes around me in so many forms! As with evening coming in the above experience, darkness can come upon me so very slowly, as a soft velvet draping cloak, and often it feels very comfortable, sometimes even comforting, to feel the folds around me. I can only imagine that the adversary is the one holding the ends of that cloak; and placing it over me would enjoy my taking on the fullness of that mantle. Now before you also get comfortable in this cloak of darkness and lost in denial, realize that since we, as believers, are promised that we "are not of night nor of darkness" that, in time, I believe, God will allow the Truth of His reality to come to us. With this in mind, you may want to answer the major theological question of this article…

What does a spiritual baseball "pitch to the cranium" feel like?

"We are neither of night nor of darkness…"
- I Thessalonians 5:6

Day 12

There's Nothing Like Unique Advice From…
Miss Perceptions

You've probably heard of "Dear Abby," Helpful Hints from Heloise,", Ask Dr. Laura," or Miss Manners." However, this may or may not be your first encounter with "Miss Perceptions." Although her advice has been very extensive over many years, we have the unique opportunity to provide some of the best letters that have come across her desk.

Dear Miss Perceptions,
Before we began singing this morning in our weekly devotional time, the song leader quoted to us that: "God inhibits the praises of His people." I found this to be a disturbing thought. Although I was relieved to also know from a similar source that: "Jesus came to give us life and give it conveniently." Could you provide some insight?

Yours mindfully,
Connie Fusion

Dear Con,
I think per chance there is a unique wisdom to be gleaned from combining these two sayings. Perhaps life is not convenient for those who inhibit the praises of God's people. Also, you may want to go back and compare which version of the

Bible these were taken from. I must admit that I do not seem to recognize the exact translation. Let me know what you find.

M.P.

Dear Miss Perceptions,

As a Sunday School teacher, I was intrigued by one student's art project illustrating "The Flight From Egypt." The drawing of the airplane was very well done, but the three figures in the front of the plane were confusing to me. Do you know who they are?

Educationally yours,
T. Cheer

Dear T,

The correct rendering of this art piece should have had two figures behind the third. Those two would be Joseph and Mary. The other at the very front of the plane would have to be Pontius, the Pilot. Just for the record, Joe and Mar did arrive safely in Egypt and lived there until given the thumbs up to return to their own land. I understand they did not fly again but rather used reliable land transportation. I hope that explains their flight more completely.

M.P.

Dear Miss Perceptions,

I will be visiting a foreign dignitary. More accurately he is part of the country's royal family and I wanted to be sure to use the correct title to address him. Is the term, "Your Immenseness" the proper way to acknowledge this individual?

Largely yours,
Vis A. Ting

Dear Vis,

Although "Your Immenseness" is acceptable, you may wish to interchange it with "Your Immensity" to provide additional recognition and diversity to the conversation. In using these acknowledgments consistently with him I believe you will find that, in turn, he will address you in a unique fashion as well. When you return, please let me know how that worked out for you.

M.P.

Disclaimer: Just remember, it is always best to check the original source of information when receiving answers from Miss Perceptions.

"Then you will know the truth, and the truth will set you free."
- John 8:32

Day 13

Being Hole-y, Whole-y, or Holy?

As I was fixing two lockers on a Monday afternoon, our security director at the school I worked at, stopped by to tell me the breaking news of a gunman who entered an Amish schoolhouse in Pennsylvania and shot several children, then turned the gun on himself. The news was extremely disturbing to me, and I have thought about and prayed for the Amish community since first learning of this devastating act.

For the following two evenings I have watched the news and have continued to shake my head in disbelief. For the record, I am what I would call, a news "junkie." I want to know what is going on in the world and community, but even considering the many tragedies I have viewed being broadcast over the years; this one has made a deeper impact to my heart and mind.

As many of you know I am originally from western Pennsylvania, and while stationed in the Army, I also lived in eastern Pennsylvania for a time, not far from "Amish country." I remember driving to that area on several occasions, marveling at these people who believe so strongly that our modern way of life takes away from their deep commitment to and communion with God. Theirs appeared to be a gentle and peaceful way of life requiring great faith to be so "outside" of mainstream society. I had to wonder about my own faith while visiting among them and considered the distractions of a fast-paced life that stole away significant portions of my personal fellowship and quiet closeness to the Lord.

On one of these visits to Amish country, my friend Paula and I noticed a wooden stand along the roadside in front of a very simple home. We pulled over and parked in order to investigate and noted on each of the shelves were pies. One after another of wonderful, made-from-scratch, (does anyone really know what that means - "made-from-scratch"? What exactly is "scratch" anyway?) warm from the oven, flakey crusted pies! It was obvious that these pies were a labor of love in the making; taking much time, effort, and care. The pies were also unattended and outside by the road with only a sign that basically said: "Pies - $4.00 each. Please place the cost within the cup." I remember Paula and I looking at each other in disbelief and thinking the same thing. Anyone could come along and help themselves to any of these delicious treats for FREE since no one was here to stop them.

[Caution: Side trip down memory lane - feel free to skip this section as it has little relevance to the daily devotional other than comic relief and nostalgia.] Just to digress for a moment I must tell you that there was a Shoofly Pie among the many varieties on that stand, and Paula went absolutely "ballistic" in finding it. She had always heard they were one-of-a-kind pies and insisted that we buy the Shoofly. Now I had looked over all the pies and there were many of my favorites there... but Shoofly was a dark horse in this running... an extremely dark horse to the point of being basically invisible to my appetite. Sure, I had heard of Shoofly Pie, but didn't even know what was in it, and any dessert with the word "fly" in it just didn't sound very appetizing to me. Let me explain, also, that Paula had been an English teacher before joining the Army and could be very, very persuasive with her convincing vocabulary and debate skills. I finally had to concede the victory of the "pie battle" to her and so the $4.00 went into the cup and the Shoofly Pie was adopted. We basically got in the car and dove right into our purchase. The pie was absolutely fantastic and the sweetest tasting dessert I had ever eaten. No wonder it was named Shoofly, no insect could resist being a part of this. It was addictive to the embarrassing admission that we ate the whole thing right then and there, to the point of becoming physically ill. I am surprised that we didn't go into a sugar coma and need to be rushed to the nearest hospital for insulin. If you ever have a chance to obtain an Amish Shoofly Pie, I suggest you do so... although you may want to use moderation in your consumption. Ultimately, Paula and I were sugar energized for days!!! [OK, thanks for the train of thought running off the track for a moment. You are a gracious audience!]

How could anyone leave these wonderful homemade pies out here for any unscrupulous dessert eater to come along and easily steal one? It appeared these Amish folks were very trusting... obviously not of us or humankind per say, but rather of God.

Tonight, as I was watching television, the reporters interviewed one Amish community member after another, and I noted such grief within each of their expressions for the loss of those innocent young girls. In such a small, tight-knit community I would think that "everyone knows everyone" and would be close to each person. Closeness such as this would cause the inner pain to be very great, and greatly shared. Each Amish individual interviewed said the same basic statement indicating that they had forgiven the gunman who had taken these precious lives. One woman shared that in being forgiven through Jesus for her transgressions, how could she not forgive the transgression of this man? Each of these precious people was feeling the depth of loss; yet, they freely were forgiving as written within The Lord's Prayer: "forgive us our trespasses as we forgive those who trespass against us."

Perhaps that is the part that makes me think about and meditate more deeply about my own heart and mind. It has made me consider in the realm of spirituality and belief in the teachings of Jesus... perhaps it is not the Amish who are the "outsiders."

**"But just as He who called you is holy, so be holy in all you do; for it is written:
'Be holy, because I am holy.'"
- I Peter 1:15,16**

Day 14

What Would Jesus...Want For Christmas?

Along came the well-known words... What would Jesus do? I must admit that I do not always know what Jesus would do regarding all the circumstances I find myself in. I do know that I often see the WWJD on bumper stickers of cars and I can tell you what Jesus wouldn't do. Jesus would NOT make a right turn from the far-left lane on a 6-lane highway!

Next came the more recent offspring of the above... What would Jesus drive? There has been much speculation about this subject. He was a carpenter, so some think he would need a truck. Of course, I would take it a step further to say that it would be a white Ford F-150 with distinctive zebra stripes, since in Psalm 50:10 it states, "for every animal of the forest is mine." Others think a minivan or SUV would be the choice to carry about those 12 disciples. Honda is claiming that they would be the choice, since the disciples "all continued with one Accord" (Acts 1:14). And, of course, Chrysler (make sure to pronounce it "Christ-ler") has their own take on the subject.

Since everyone is asking these "what would Jesus" questions, and, of course, since I don't want to be excluded from such deeper levels of contemplation, I was thinking about the holidays and then combined the "what would Jesus" phrase with another season phrase.   How could I not come to the likely conclusion: What would Jesus... want for Christmas?

Now, I am sure you have heard about certain products that boast of being the gift for "the person who has everything." So, forget the McDonald's Big Mac certificates, because God "has the cattle on a thousand hills" (Psalm 50:10). We can rule out the Lexus keys given in clever ways to the recipient, as in the commercials, because God states in Psalm 50:12 that, "the world is mine, and all that is in it." Surely here is someone who does have everything. So, what's a gift giver to do? I believe the woman who visits Jesus while he is having dinner at a Pharisee's home has the perfect holiday gift solution... and it is not a Martha Stewart exclusive.

Picture this... Jesus is sitting down to the dinner table with some very important and devout religious folks, known as Pharisees. These are people who do all the right things, in all the right places, with all the right people, and follow all the right rules. Next enters a... lady... who, let's say, happens to be from the "red torch" (since lights were not invented yet) district of the town.

Anyway... this woman came into the room and while Jesus was sitting at the table, she wept over his feet, bathing them with her tears. Please realize this had to be a rather significant amount of crying, because she was next drying his feet with her hair. Then, taking it a step further, she poured a very expensive perfume over them as well. Above everything, she was doing this rather humbling interaction in front of a group of people who really did not think very highly of her, as reflected in the verse, "If this man (Jesus) were a prophet, he would know who is touching him and what kind of woman she is - that she is a sinner." Jesus then reminded Simon that she had given him all the things that Simon had not: "I came into your house. You did not give me any water for my feet, but she wet my feet with her tears and wiped them with her hair. You did not give me a kiss, but this woman from the time I entered has not stopped kissing my feet. You did not put oil on my head, but she has poured perfume on my feet" (Luke 7:44-46). She gave the gifts that the host of this gathering had neglected to give.

In the most symbolic way imaginable, this woman gave Jesus a most wonderful gift - all of herself, the best and the worst, totally and completely. Perhaps we should put a bow over our hearts this Christmas season and give Jesus the most unique gift that can only come from each one of us... ourselves.

"And hope does not disappoint; because the love God has been poured out within our hearts through the Holy Spirit who was given to us."
- Romans 5:2

Day 15

Sister Mary Bovine

As most of you know, I was raised Catholic and even after coming to a personal relationship with Jesus I had taken time to look at about every Protestant denomination in existence and found the differences and variety to be staggering to say the least. In that overwhelming state of decision-making I continued being Catholic and then wondered if perhaps that this coming to Jesus as Lord and Savior was "the calling." For Catholics "the calling" is when one believes that he/she has a vocation as a priest or nun and so I decided to pursue this line of thinking by spending a week with a group of nuns called The Maryvale Sisters. Please note that I tried joining the convent, but it did not work out for me. In summary, I thought I had the calling, but it was the wrong number.

The Maryvale Sisters are a very small group of nuns, who own a very large farm and run a school just outside of Charlotte, North Carolina. I was shown the various tasks that were needed to run the farm and learned quickly about feeding the very shy goat, taking care of the many rabbit hutches, picking the vegetables in the garden, watering the cows, and especially finding the eggs which were laid in every section of the barn by some very enterprising chickens each day. I would climb the bales of hay to the top of the barn and back down each morning; combing each inch on a thorough Easter egg hunt provided by very undisciplined chickens. I am sure I heard clucks of laughter as I was on morning egg patrol. Obviously, chickens are easily amused.

It was such a morning that one of the sisters asked me to accompany her into the nearby town to visit the bakery shop. These nuns made the most wholesome foods I had ever eaten, so I was surprised that we would even consider going to such a place of sugar and sweets. I helped load the pick-up truck with a variety of many days old bread, buns, and other desserts, some of which were not something I personally wanted to consume. To be very frank, some of the baked goods could be renamed baked "bads" and looked like the beginnings of a penicillin experiment which only Sir Alexander Fleming (the discoverer of penicillin) would have found even somewhat interesting. Sister then explained to me that this was quite a treat for the cows and that they were going to be the consumers of this bakery bonanza.

We returned to the farm, loaded the wheel barrel with the goodies, and went inside the fence into cow territory. Now the only cows I had ever seen were at a distance such as driving on the Pennsylvania turnpike and observing the rolling hills with the creatures which looked so quaint, so picturesque, so... small. Sister explained that she and I would be handing out the "spoils" to the cows so that all of them would get a fair share while keeping some semblance of order in the feeding. It seemed easy enough and I noted that the entire herd was way in the distance, a mere speck on the horizon. I jumped when sister suddenly and without warning yelled as loud as she could, "bossy, bossy, bossy" and the small dots in the distance began moving and moving quite rapidly. The cows began getting larger upon approach and it was then that I realized just how huge "bossy" and his or her friends really were. I also realized that there were many of them. And I noticed they were heading right for us. I remembered those old cowboy movies where the herd suddenly gets out of control and I wanted to scream "stampede" and run for my life, because deep inside there was this increasing fear building. I glanced at Sister and she was standing calmly waiting. Not wanting to show my inner terror, I did likewise even though my mind was repeating the news flash; "Nun and visitor trampled by mad cows over dessert... details at 11." (Please note that when I use the term "mad" cows I am referring to their temperament and not the now publicized disease in which a bovine in the latter stages of the illness imitates erratic dance moves).

Before I knew it, we were surrounded, and the cows were being rather "pushy". I tried pushing back but it was like bumping against an SUV in a school carpool line, and I was still fearing being in the middle of this herd. Bravely, I moved to stand next to sister. I was pressing against her to save me from the impending doom I was expecting. She glanced at me and said, "If they bother you... just smack them on the nose and they will back up." I wish I could tell you that I was able to follow her instruction but instead I just basically remained safely against her and allowed her to do the cow crowd control. I watched her handle the herd very effectively and my fears diminished just remaining with her. I even came to really look at those cows with such soulful eyes and velvet noses and how even they seemed to know that this nun was leader of the pack… or herd in this case.

In recalling this adventure, I thought of times that I have been surrounded by impending circumstances that have caused such deep fears. Even when I know I should "smack" whatever is impinging upon me, I find that I am unable to do so. That is when I remember Sister Mary Bovine and know that there is One who I can go and lean on to be safe, knowing that Jesus is in control of all that surrounds me. I keep coming back to attempting to trusting Him more in my life. I hope you feel free to do the same!

> **"But I will rescue you on that day, declares the Lord;**
> **you will not be handed over to those you fear."**
> **- Jeremiah 39:17**

Day 16

The Gift For The One Who Has Everything

I am sure we all are familiar with the ever-popular phrase during the Christmas season: "What do you get the person who has everything?" Often, we are bombarded with this ideation by endless commercials nearly demanding that we buy some unique piece of expensive jewelry, after all "HE went to Jared!" Even on television, the diamond displayed is sparkling and blinding as light beams are aimed with precision at just the right angle to dazzle the consumer who most likely is filled with guilt (you know guilt, the gift that keeps on giving) for not having considered such a precious, one-of-a-kind gift. After all, "every kiss begins with Kay," "a diamond is forever", and don't forget that at The Shane Company "you have a friend in the diamond business." I know I feel much closer to Mr. Shane after hearing that we are now "friends." How about I stop by and ask him for an interest free loan on one of those diamond pendants, eh? In the end, I bet we're not that close of friends, now are we?

The other gift that seems aimed at the person who has everything is the expensive car sitting out in front of someone's home with a HUGE red bow on top. I used to ask myself, "Does this really happen in real life? Does someone really buy a car and put a big bow on it as a gift?" Yes, Virginia, it does happen because when I lived in Lawrenceville one of my neighbor's did the "car with the bow on top" gift. Just for the record, it wasn't a Lexis... it was a Toyota Corolla... but really, isn't it the thought that counts? Perhaps not, for the person who has everything.

Then again, is there anyone who really has everything? Does God have everything? After all there is the scripture which states: "The earth is the Lord's, and everything in it, the world, and all who live in it." (Psalm 24:1). With that in mind I must admit that last Christmas I sat down and asked myself: If I were going to give Jesus a gift for Christmas (which would be a birthday present) what would it be? What do you give God, who really does have everything?

I first thought that if I were not a believer already, I could give myself/my life to Him. But I did that back in 1973, not at Christmas, but still I did give my life to Him, so He already had that… or… did He? I remember how I knew nothing about "Christian culture" when I accepted Jesus as Savior and each day, after making my commitment to the Lord, was a revelation. I had no expectations of how He would answer prayer; and, I really didn't even know how to pray. I would just talk to Jesus, almost constantly, after all, He was alive, real, and listening. That was amazing, that He was always listening to me, even when I woke up at 3:00 am. Instead of tossing and turning to go back to sleep, Jesus and I would just "have ourselves a little talk." And then I realized that over the 30 some years since Jesus and I met, I had expectations of how He should answer my prayers. Now I knew the "proper" way to pray, after all I had prayed in small groups and listened to more experienced believers talk to God. I learned all the Christian vocabulary after asking many questions from those same experienced believers over the years. The night I came to make a commitment to God, those around me were saying I was "saved," "born-again," "a Christian," and that Christ was "in my heart" (which, when I pictured it in my head, seemed rather odd, especially if I was having a bout of heartburn). I had no idea what any of that meant, I only knew that something changed… or rather someone changed, and that someone was me. I knew when I walked out of the room where I had prayed the prayer of salvation, that I was really loved by God, that He died for my sins, that forgiveness had been given, and that an adventure had begun.

But… as the years went by, I noticed that God didn't really surprise me much anymore. I don't believe God stopped doing wonders in my life, I just had "expectations" about how all this was "supposed" to work. As I have heard from those married for many years, perhaps I also had come to take God for granted. I knew from other believers what to expect, how to pray, and I became what I refer to as a "professional Christian." Everything had become rather, I suppose the appropriate word would be "routine." Somehow, I didn't want a routine Christmas last year which led to this whole topic of what gift to give to God.

A few days ago, I happened to be looking for my dog, Georgie, in my bedroom closet (that's another story for another day) and I found my gift to God from last Christmas. It was a simple red stocking filled with many items which were symbolic of different things that I wanted to "rededicate" to God. In breaking down parts of my life and self with different symbols, it seemed to mean more than just making the blanket statement of, "Lord, I rededicate my life to you." (blah, blah, blah... another blanket statement without much depth). In retrospect as I pulled out each item, it forced me to think about how much of that part of me did I really give to God over the past year? Some parts I gave a great deal or all, and, in others, I didn't give much, or perhaps took that area back totally. It caused me to take the time to really consider each area of my life more fully and meditate over events and my response to them over the past year. It was out of the ordinary, it was unique, it was... my first step in trying not to take God for granted.

I thought that last year was interesting in finding symbolic items to fill the stocking, but this year it meant more to open it with Jesus and "have a talk" about what I really had given to, or taken back from, God. It may be good to have "a friend in the diamond business," but it's even better to have "a Friend in the heart business."

So, this Christmas... what are you getting for the One who has everything?

"The earth is the Lord's, and everything in it, the world, and all who live in it."
- Psalm 24:1

37

Day 17

How The Grinch Stole… Convenience

I thought yesterday was going to be a normal day. I woke up and went through my morning routine of showering, dressing, preparing, and so on. I packed up my feathered friend/parrot, Galileo, and got her situated in my truck being sure the seat belt was fastened on her. Let me clarify that the seat belt is fastened around her CAGE, not her personally. To do that would be to risk losing a finger or two. But please note that even Galileo buckles up for safety and so should you. (This is a public service announcement from the Highway Safety Council and the author.) In any case, Galileo can be quite the role model, but I digress from my story.

Next, I got in my truck and adjusted everything… seatbelt and all, placed the key in the ignition, and turned it. The entire morning changed in just that one moment, as there was no sound of an engine trying to turn over. Unfortunately, there was no engine activity at all, just that sickening sound of click, click, click. Now, I really do not know a lot about car engines, but I always feel I need to look under the hood just to be sure it isn't something simple. Perhaps a fuse blew, a belt broke, or a wire came loose. In this case I thought the battery terminals may have been corroded. To my dismay they were fine. If only the trouble were so simple, but alas, it was not to be.

As I began to make phone calls to solve my dilemma, it really hit me… what a convenience this technological wonder is. Here I was holding this tiny phone in my hand, as I called the cavalry to come and rescue me. If only Custer had a cell phone in his time of crisis or those at the Alamo. Could history itself have been written differently? There are so many technological wonders in life, many bordering on the miraculous. They make life so much easier; but, just how easy should my life be? Is it possible that convenience could be counter-productive?

I wonder how many of these things we see as conveniences, technological or otherwise, change the course of our personal history. Should my history be changed by convenience? I began to think through some of the conveniences that are in my life and could I live without them? As a society and culture, it seems if it takes less effort, less time, and less brain effort… it must be a good thing. After all, why would anyone want to tire him/herself physically or mentally? Who would want to spend too much time doing a task? Times like these that are too obvious seem to make me question the validity of what the norm or accepted trend in life is. My truck breaking down was no exception.

Now don't get me wrong, I am very grateful for our advances. I am very thankful for indoor plumbing, running water, my car and my computer. But I find it interesting that I must make an effort to do more physical activities in order to prevent health issues and problems that may arise. I "go for a walk," much like the dog does, without the collar and leash of course. But I don't often walk somewhere on purpose. Instead, I drive to places that are necessary destinations. I can work in the yard and usually find muscles that haven't been used as much as they should. Perhaps I need to go to the gym to work on those areas that don't get used much. How many times do I trade convenience for my own health and well-being? Ultimately, I must MAKE a conscious decision to take care of myself physically. In looking at how stressful life has become; the same purposeful decision-making involves my mental well-being also. How many of us actually take time to reflect on our decisions, our life, where we are going… which takes a conscious effort. Shouldn't that be convenient also? I think perhaps there are some areas of life that we need to make the decision to work through certain aspects of ourselves.

It will not be easy. It won't be convenient. It won't be a quick fix. It will take commitment. It will take resolve. It will be a challenge. It means that I could fail, and society certainly has taught us that is one of the most horrible things that can happen to us in life. Ultimately some things that are good and necessary for our well-being will NEVER really be… *gasp*… convenient… EVER!!!

I can only compare it with how it must have felt to have Christmas come even after the Grinch stole all the presents from Whoville. It came without wrappings, it came without decorations, and it came without presents, boxes, or bows. Why it even came without the Who Pudding or the Roast Beast! All of Whoville learned a valuable lesson, as well as I. Even without the trappings of convenience, and with the additional requirement of effort… a much deeper meaning may be discovered in all that we endeavor to do.

"O Lord, be gracious to us; we long for you.
Be our strength every morning, our salvation in time of distress."
- Isaiah 33:2

Day 18

"It's A Matter Of Life And Death"

I have heard that phrase said before, but not very seriously. Usually it has been used when someone wants to emphasize that a situation is very important to them, and they need my immediate attention regarding that particular matter. It had never really involved someone on the precipice between life and death. However, for some places, such as Tanzania, Africa, this phrase describes their everyday reality. Let me share with you two special people who God placed in my life while in Africa.

The first individual is Florence. She was a 27-year-old woman with AIDS who I was asked to visit by, Mary, a social worker in the village of Karanse. From the description of Florence, it was apparent that she was extremely ill. I gathered together all the medical supplies that were needed, and we went to visit her in the outskirts of the village. I have been with dying patients before, but not in a setting such as this. The "house" we arrived at was a concrete block building divided into two small rooms. There was one window without glass, and a doorway without a door covered only with a piece of cloth reaching from top to bottom. The chickens located around the house would enter and leave through the doorway at will.

Florence was lying upon a low wooden plywood "bed," located below the window opening, with a thin foam rubber mattress to cushion her frail frame. She was very thin, many sores covered her body, her breathing was labored, and pesky flies were numerous in the dim lighting that came through the window. The only

41

help I could give was to make her as comfortable as possible; yet, I can only describe my efforts as "fighting a leopard with a toothpick."

Florence's mother had been caring for her and had done a good job, especially considering how few provisions she had. I showed and described each step of what I was doing so that she could continue caring for her daughter with the supplies I had brought. After I was done, I asked if I could pray with Florence. She could not speak over a whisper but indicated that I could. I knelt and took her thin hand in mine, noting that Mary had come to kneel beside me, and Florence's mother next to Mary. There was something about that moment that seemed to transcend time and place... perhaps it was a very precious closeness of Jesus that came into that dark room. Where our efforts seemed so very small and limited, how much bigger God was as I prayed. When I paused between each sentence of my prayer, Mary translated into Swahili, and then Florence's mother translated into another language... a local dialect or perhaps Masai. I did not know for sure, but even hearing my simple prayer repeated into two other tongues reminded me of Pentecost. I know that it was not a particularly long prayer, but time appeared to stand still, and eternity had become a reality.

In finishing, I told Florence that I would be back tomorrow as the three of us walked out of the house together. I informed Florence's mother that I would bring more supplies, since I had used most of the provisions and wanted to be sure that she had more on hand. We hugged, and she thanked me... I told her I was glad to come.

The next morning the social worker purchased a "wash" which we would use to bathe Florence that would help soothe her skin and deter the flies. However, it was cool and breezy at that time of day, so we decided to wait until after lunch when it would be warmer. After eating we were gathering together the supplies when a neighbor came on his bicycle to the school and informed us that... Florence had died about an hour earlier. The news came as a "punch in the gut" and something I had not even prepared myself to consider. I knew that Florence would die... I knew what she had was not curable... but I did not expect it to be the day after visiting her.

The next morning, we returned to the school and I set up my "health clinic" on the porch outside one of the classrooms. It was then that Kelvin, an 8-year-old student, was brought to me. His teacher said that Kelvin was not feeling well and after an assessment it was apparent that he was ill, especially with a temperature of

42

101 degrees. The teacher indicated that we needed to go to the Compassion Office in the village for Kelvin to be taken to the hospital, and, so, I accompanied Kelvin there. However, the office was locked and there was no one there.

We were advised by another teacher that the Compassion worker should be back shortly, and we waited about 30 minutes or so. Kelvin was feeling worse and anxious as we were waiting. It seemed best for us to return to the school. Arriving there, I spoke with the pastor, who sponsors the school, and our driver, explaining that Kelvin needed medical attention. After taking his temperature again, it was now 102 degrees, indicating that he was getting worse. It was then that the pastor instructed our driver to take Kelvin to the hospital. Knowing that Kelvin was on his way to receive treatment, I returned to my "porch clinic." I felt that perhaps it was a case of malaria, but we had caught it in the early stages and Kelvin would get the medication he needed.

About an hour later the pastor returned to tell me that after Kelvin arrived at the hospital and as they were assessing his condition, he went into convulsions. The medical staff worked quickly to stabilize him and if it would have been 15 minutes longer... Kelvin would have died.

After hearing this... I had to sit down! I was totally overwhelmed! One of the school teachers from Karanse said to me later "You have brought a miracle." But I could only reply: "God is good, and it is His miracle. This is beyond my doing. I am humbled by all that has happened in being here."

I am grateful that the Lord has allowed me to be a part of His Work in Tanzania. The impact of it all has been life changing. I can only repeat what is written in God's Word: "You hem me in, behind and before; You have laid Your Hand upon me. Such knowledge is too wonderful for me, too lofty for me to attain." - Psalm 139:5,6

Always know that God has His Hand upon each of us, and that is truly a wonderful gift!

"He performs wonders that cannot be fathomed, miracles that cannot be numbered."
- Job: 9:10

43

Day 19

A Prayer For One Of THOSE Days

Ever have one of THOSE days? You have struggled and figured and thought and rehearsed and relived and argued and reviewed and... and... and nothing was making sense... nothing was being resolved and it all seemed an endless maze of confusion.

Have you ever had one of THOSE days?
(Please note: This is the closest to poetry that I will ever attempt so if you are not into poetry, feel free to skip this page. As you can see, it doesn't even rhyme. ::grin::)

In and of myself, I have nothing left for anyone around me... not anything for myself... not even for God, so it seemed.

And from the depths of that loss within, and that total overwhelming from without came this prayer:

What have I done?
I have reduced You from Embracing Compassion to paper gospels and goals impersonal, dependent upon me.
Reduced You to my smallness, such limited finite figures that add up only to selfish humanness.

Nothing but a list of attributes that are actions alone
to build into another tower, that tries to reach You.
But it should be toppled.

Razed to the ground, where I sit in the center wondering... what should not have
been.
Sitting in the rubble looking at the destruction
wondering what happened.
All wrong,
all wrongly built in Your Name.
And without You ... all I have built is lacking.

Not by my hands to be built... but Yours.
Pierced Hands moving into mine
and I watch as they come alive in a different way,
in true Life,
in life Truth,
in that Way... only your Way... only in your Way.
Depth of Life to be embraced
Embrace me.

I find it interesting how one of days puts everything around me into a new and
life-giving perspective that can come only from Jesus. It doesn't get much more
personal than that.

"Mercy, peace, and love be yours in abundance."
- Jude 1:2

Day 20

Got Turkey?

It was a simple invitation, completed by the young hands of a first grader. It was Thanksgiving and the first grade at the school where I was employed had invited me to their Thanksgiving feast. Well, how could I resist? The invitation itself was a work of art, labored over so completely, as was obvious. A few misspelled words added to the realism of the age of the creator. In addition, part of the invitation asked that I, as the recipient, should consider whether I wished to dress for the occasion as a Pilgrim or an Indian/ Native American. I pondered whom I wished to be and came to an impasse, which seems silly for a woman in her maturing years. Did I just admit that I am mature? Others would most likely argue that observation, as some days, I would also. But...I digress.

I began to think if there was anyone else who came to that first Thanksgiving feast and alas, I did think of one other. A most important character indeed and a vital component of the whole celebration... the turkey!!!! Now who in their right mind would ever want to come as the "turkey?" What implications would that have, especially for the one doing the dressing as such a creature?

The turkey... hmmm... well, on the one hand I would be the center of the feast, but, then, would I really want to be in such an insulting role. No one else, I was reasonably sure, would be willing to do so, if they had even thought of the idea. Even the title, TURKEY, well, it has negative connotations. To attend as a large bird, or rather, to be more precise, a FAT bird was not very flattering. But, after all, wasn't that the purpose since it was for dinner? In addition, I have heard it said that turkeys are not the most intelligent of beings, although I have not had any direct contact with one for an extended period of time. Then there is the use of the term itself which can be used as an insult..."You turkey!" That indicates that we hold the person in rather low esteem. Looking over all these implications it would seem that to be a turkey, even for a Thanksgiving feast, would jeopardize my very self-esteem and make me appear foolish. Why would anyone want to do that?

I concluded that if I could find a turkey costume to rent then I would consider the matter further, despite the insulting ramifications. Guess what? I found one at the first costume shop I visited, and it was quite a comical, happy looking rendition of a turkey. I fell in love with it at first sight! It truly was the essence of joy in appearance and there was no way anyone could look at this creature and not smile. I decided that I would be glad to be dressed in this special costume despite the consequences. I rented it on the spot.

The day of the feast came, and I placed the outfit on not realizing how large and cumbersome it would be. I had to take large, long steps so as not to trip over the huge three toed feet over my own (which do have five toes just for the record). Not only was I looking the part, but I had to be clumsy and awkward even in my movements, adding to the overall "turkey" persona. I remember walking into the room and there was silence for a moment before the place irrupted with cheering, yelling and waving. Several children left their seats and came to hug me. The teachers were thrilled as well since who would have expected the guest of honor at Thanksgiving to come to their very feast. It was a moment I will NEVER forget since the joy and happiness that they all felt and expressed came back to me a hundred-fold.

Since that day, when times have come about with individuals that are too serious and tension seems to be most thick in the very air around us, I think of that Thanksgiving feast and my "being the turkey." Any humiliation that may have invaded me in being considered a turkey is well worth the price to see another be able to smile and see things on a lighter note, even at the risk to my own self esteem. That special Thanksgiving feast has strengthened my knowing who I truly am... a turkey perhaps on the outside, but a very caring person inside who wants to make another smile.

Can I get a "gobble, gobble?"

"Rejoice always; pray without ceasing; in everything give thanks."
- I Thessalonians 5:17, 18

Day 21

Which Do You Want First...The Good News Or The Bad News?

I remember the saying as a child, "When dog bites man, that isn't news; but, when man bites dog – now that's news!" Keeping this in mind when I owned a parrot, I was interested in a bumper sticker which said: "Happiness is biting your parrot back." One day when my parrot, Galley, bit me very hard, I thought I would follow the wisdom of the bumper sticker. So, with teeth exposed, I came at the little feather-ball who proceeded to defend herself by grabbing one tooth with her powerful beak and hung on with the force of a pair of plyers. Realizing that I may have an unexpected visit from the tooth fairy, I backed up while prying Galley off my face. The good news for me is that my tooth stayed in my mouth, and the good news for my parrot was that I never tried to bite her again. The bad news, as we learned, was not to believe everything we read about what constitutes news or even happiness, especially when it involves a bumper sticker.

Another example involves a man with a history of heart problems who had been to the hospital the day before and received an EKG. He was to take the information about the EKG to his doctor to interpret the results. Now he was frantically looking for the report which had somehow been misplaced in the house. Finally, he asked his wife if she had seen the EKG. "Yes, dear," she replied, "as a matter of fact I did. But which do you want first the good news or the bad news?" Bewildered at the question, he hesitatingly said, "The good news I think." To this the wife responded, "I found your EKG sitting on the player piano in the den this morning."

"Thank goodness," the man replied with obvious relief, then nonchalantly added, "So what's the bad news?" "Well," she explained, "I thought your EKG was a new roll of music for the player piano, so I put it in for a listen. Honey, I don't know how to put this delicately... but it played the song... Nearer My God To Thee!"

So, what is news anyway? It appears to involve something unique or out of the ordinary, something not expected... like man biting a dog, an owner biting a parrot, or a parrot doing dental surgery. Depending on your perspective, news may be of two persuasions: good or bad.

How you view them, now that's a separate issue.

**"It is because of Him that you are in Christ Jesus,
who has become for us wisdom from God
– that is, our righteousness, holiness and redemption."
- I Corinthians 1:30**

Day 22

The History Of: "Dear John"

In my vast explorations and education in Sociology and Anthropology, I have come upon the first penned "Dear John" letter in history. Oddly enough it was written to the Bible persona, John the Baptist. I thought it would be advantageous to share this unique find with all of you.

Dear John:

I had heard rumors regarding your new activities, but certainly did not believe any of it. How could I believe that my dearest boyfriend moved from his childhood home and took up residence in, dare I even say it??? The wilderness!!!!! What do you expect to accomplish in such a place, except to receive endless sunburns, be thirsty all the time, and totally alone? How could you even consider such a thing? What are you thinking?????

Didn't you hear what your father told you over all those years of growing up? Your father saw an ANGEL in the temple that foretold of the great man you would become throughout the years of your life. You are the one to go before and make a way for the long-awaited Messiah to our Hebrew people!!! How are you expecting to do that while living in a rock and sand strewn desert???? You are in the wilderness, and it is called that for a reason, John... no one CHOOSES to live in such a stark environment, unless perhaps he has lost his mind! You appeared to be rational when the two of us attended that wedding feast a few weeks ago.

Although, now that I think about it further, you were rather quiet and so very… calm, perhaps a better term would be…peaceful. I had thought it was because you were considering the position offered to you in the temple, much like the vocation your father had faithfully carried out. After all, John, you are from a priestly tribe and what greater HONOR is there than serving in the temple!!! I cannot believe you are throwing it all away to live in the desert, like some wild animal.

I understand that Hannah went out to see you and she has confirmed all of this to me. She said you look like a madman wearing camel's hair clothing. And if that were not enough, she reported that you are eating insects… locusts of all things!!! How could you possibly stomach such vile, crawling, disgusting creatures??? Are you even sure they are kosher regarding our dietary laws? She said that your entire diet consisted of those horrible insects and wild honey. That's all you are eating???? How do you expect to even survive, in the desert no less, on only those two means of sustenance??? You will starve to death with so little!

Hannah also said that you are telling people to repent and turn from their sinful ways. John, no one will be open to such rhetoric. No one wants to be told they are a sinner, and who are you to judge them?? And what is this idea of baptizing people who are misguided enough to come to the desert to see you? Using water to symbolize that they have changed their lives!!! How did you ever invent such a strange concept??? All of this is total and complete nonsense!!!!!

John, can you not see the folly of all of this? You are going to MISS your calling that was spoken from the angel!!! No one will come out to the wilderness to be baptized. Why would anyone allow others to know what evil things they have done… and coming to you, John, to be baptized, means admitting such things out loud to the entire world. Hannah admitted that she tried to reason with you, to persuade you to return to "the real world" but, that you see this as your mission and calling in life… that you are resolute in staying. All I can say is that you are throwing your life away.

I fear there is nothing that any of us, including myself, will be able to do or say to convince you to turn from this folly. Therefore, I am going to have to consider our relationship as coming to an end. As much as I love you, John, I cannot consider a future with someone who chooses to do something so unconventional. I understand your cousin, Jesus, has begun to speak publicly and his message is beginning to attract a small gathering. Perhaps you should consider being more like him.

I wish you well John, although I believe you are making a terrible mistake with your life. I expect things to come to tragedy for you. Shalom, John.

Fondly,
Abigail

So… where is God leading you?

> **"I tell you the truth:**
> **Among those born of women there has not risen**
> **anyone greater than John the Baptist;**
> **yet he who is least in the kingdom of heaven is greater than he."**
> **– Matthew 11:11**

Day 23

A Chicken Or Pig Perspective: You Just Never Know

One morning a chicken and a pig were walking down the street in a large metropolitan area. Both stopped abruptly as they saw a line of individuals who were waiting to get a free meal at one of the local mission shelters. Both felt compassion for these unfortunate people and the pig was the first to express his concern.

"Look at those poor people. I wish there was a way we could help them." The chicken nodded in agreement and then suddenly became excited, enthusiastically stating, "Hey! I know what we can do to help. Let's give them a ham and eggs breakfast!!!" The pig looked at the chicken discerningly and explained, "Yeah, that's easy for you to suggest. For you it's just a freewill offering, but, for me, it's total commitment!"

Sometimes our perspective of a situation does much to define it... for us. But, often, we have no concept of what the impact will be for another.

This was true for a Veterans Day Program I attended several years ago. Invitations were sent which resulted in three active duty soldiers from Ft. McPherson attending, since their commanding officer had another program to be present for at the same time. Basically, in Army terms, it meant they "had" to attend our program and really did not expect it to be "significant," but rather, just another "duty" to be carried out.

However, the sergeant who came with this group had been in the Vietnam War, as well as the conflicts in the Middle East. He told me how there was no "welcome home" upon his return from Vietnam and that, for him, no one cared about his military service, especially in Vietnam... until now. He explained that our program and the appreciation we expressed was the "homecoming" he never received. Later, I was informed by someone sitting nearby during the main program, that when those on active duty were asked to stand, this sergeant broke down sobbing, prompting one of his colleagues to place a comforting arm around him. Coming to our Veterans Day Program became more than just a "duty," but a time of honoring this soldier, and it came just 6 months before his retirement from the military.

In like manner, the captain from this group spoke to me of the many experiences that touched her life. One of the hardest parts to hear was how she returned from Iraq and only one of her friends was at the airport to welcome her back. Our program touched her in a very deep way. At the time of "passing the microphone" when the veterans were sharing their stories, she had tears in her eyes as she spoke and ended in stating, "This may be just another school function for you, but it's something I will remember the rest of my life."

So... as with the chicken and the pig, it seems we never know when God will take our simplest "freewill offering" and transform it to mean a "total commitment" for those around us.

"I thank my God every time I remember you."
- Philippians 1:3

Day 24

For Blessings To Fly

I had been thinking and praying about this devotional and what to write about next. Sure, I had a few ideas, but they were just not coming about fully. Sunday afternoon rolled around, and I was still rather blank. With some urgent matters pressing at the beginning of this week I tried to write this part before the end of the weekend. So, for me, the eleventh hour was approaching quickly.

To clear my mind, I decided to go jogging Sunday afternoon and went to the school track nearby to do so. I started around lap two and noticed a dad with two children in the field nearby about to fly a kite. It was very windy on Sunday and the perfect day for a March kite flight. It seemed all too perfect. As I finished up my last lap, I noticed that the kite was still not in the air. Hmmm… I wondered if they needed someone to hold the kite or to do the running of it, so I went over and offered my assistance. During each try the contraption only spun out of control. After further inspection we discovered that one of the rods down the side had broken, so that one side could not stay taunt and, therefore, could not get airborne. I told them to wait a minute while I went to my truck to get something.

I returned with a kite. Yes, strangely enough while others carry a jack and spare tire, I also carry a kite in my vehicle. It was a birthday gift from my brother many years ago and has lasted through many windy trips at the beach of Tybee Island, Georgia, flying over the ocean. In all those years of flying it seemed I lost the crossbar to keep the nylon stretched in place. But we looked at the broken kite and found another bar that fit perfectly in the place of the missing piece. In a couple of minutes that kite was up and flying high and two very excited children were taking turns at the helm.

The gentleman looked at me and said, "I never expected this. What are the chances of you being here jogging, coming over to help, having a kite with you, and that the crossbar would fit for the lost one? This is amazing!" I could only agree it was very amazing, indeed. Let me say that I am not amazed at God and his ways and timing. They are perfect always. But what does amaze me is when I play a part in God's amazing scenarios, even those as simple as flying a kite.

Certainly, I do not understand how any of these things come together since God's ways are greater than mine. But I am beginning to understand more and more that the time I take for others even in the simplest ways becomes a wonderful blessing. I had so many errands to do after jogging and a long list of items to be checked off. I love flying kites and suppose that is why one is in my truck. I wanted to see that one flying with those two kids and have them enjoy the experience. Perhaps it is something they will all remember the next time they have a chance to help another person. Perhaps I will always remember that taking time for others is a very direct blessing from God... and that blessing may become a wonderful subject for the page of a book.

To all of you... please don't miss the blessing either.

"Surely you have granted him eternal blessings and made him
glad with the joy of your presence."
- Psalm 21:6

Day 25

I Am Buzz Lightyear… I Come In Peace (or is it pieces?)

There is nothing quite like a Buzz Lightyear action figure. If you don't know who he is, this is a question your children most likely can field. Yes, Buzz Lightyear sits on my desk. Why? Good question. The one unexpected perk that Buzz has brought is that my status has increased just for owning one. He obviously is a trend setter, a hero to many, and an all-around "good guy." But that isn't the "real" reason he sits on my desk.

Hopefully you have seen the movie *Toy Story*. If not, I highly recommend it even if you're an adult, after all, we all know adults are just "big kids" in adult clothing anyway. Do you remember that Buzz believed that he was THE Buzz Lightyear, Space Ranger? Even with Woody in his face proclaiming "you're just a toy" he isn't convinced until… the television commercial!!! Reality check!!! But as one last attempt Buzz climbs onto the railing of the staircase, puts out his wings, and aims for that open window. And with all his might… he tries to fly but falls to the landing below with his arm broken off… his lights still blinking as he lays unconscious. The next scene is ole Buzz dressed in a hat and apron, being call Mrs. Nesmith, and having tea with the "Marie Antoinette Sisters." When Woody finally finds him, poor Buzz is insisting he really is Mrs. Nesmith and raving about how good he looks in the hat; the apron, however, he concludes was a "bit much." Does this guy have an identity crisis or what? However, between Woody, Sid's toys (or whatever mutant sort of creations they were), and the goal of returning to Andy;

58

Buzz comes to the conclusion and realization that he is Buzz Lightyear, Space Ranger THE TOY.

So now you're saying to yourself, that was an interesting story but what does it have to do with anything? That's what I said too, but then I went back and saw the movie again. I concluded that I have at times tried to be who I'm not, tried to be what others want me to be, tried to meet unrealistic expectations... maybe I even tried to be what I "thought" God wanted me to be instead of the creation He has made me to be. Like Buzz, I ended up jumping off dangerously high places that I shouldn't or looked in the mirror wondering why I was wearing a goofy-looking hat and apron. I think I've even had tea with a few headless folks somewhere along the way. Why? I'm not sure. But I need to begin with the truth of who I really am, just as Buzz began with who he was – not the super-duper, action space hero; but rather the genuine, one and only real self that Buzz is and that I am. At that starting point and with that honesty, I believe with God's help, I can go "to infinity and beyond."

> **"Therefore, whoever humbles himself like this child is the greatest in the kingdom of heaven."**
> **- Matthew 18:4**

Day 26

The Proper Distance In The Convoy Of Life

It was my first time driving in a convoy at night and I had just learned how to drive my Army jeep only a few weeks before going "to the field." The part that made this more interesting for me was that I had, during those days of learning to shift gears on a manual transmission, stalled the jeep in the middle of the busiest intersection of the German town I was stationed at in the Army. May I say that I learned many new German words that day from the other drivers who were caught in the traffic jam that I had caused that day. It was certainly memorable for ALL of us!

Driving a military vehicle at night is very different than driving a civilian car. Civilians use headlights to see and Army vehicles use blackout lights. Instead of headlights which illuminate very well, the jeep had slits of light with a hood that would keep it from being seen from above, which is an excellent idea so that enemy aircraft flying over will not be able to see, in this case, an Army jeep. The light from these slits is not very bright and to be sure that you maintained a safe distance from the military vehicle in front of you, there was a device on the back of each that you would follow. The tricky part of this device required you to pay attention to the two lights that were illuminated there, and, in doing so, you would maintain a safe distance. To be specific, there were two bars that would be showing, one red and one white. The idea was to keep those two bars of light at the same brightness as you were following the vehicle in front of you. If you got too far behind, the one light (I think it was the white one, but it has been a while since I have done this, so,

60

don't quote me) would become less bright because of the distance increasing between the vehicles. If you got too close the one light (again, the white one, I believe) would become very bright because of the decreasing distance. In other words, the BALANCE in brightness between the two lights was the key to keeping the proper distance.

I was thinking about this recently when I came to realize that I need to keep my gaze and concentration steady when following what God would have me to do as well. If I get too far behind from God's leading, then it is likely I will miss out on what He has for me and be lost as He moves on, losing sight of His Plan. On the other hand, if I get too close, I may very well just pass Him by altogether and go off on my own, not even doing what He has, but instead doing what I "think" is His Plan. In both cases, I will end up MISSING the leading of God and end up on my own... which in enemy territory could be a very dangerous situation.

I pray that in the following of God's leading in our lives, we may all be watching for and concentrating on the balance of His Light in all that we do!

"We are not of night nor of darkness..."
- I Thessalonians 5:5

Day 27

The Top 14 Lessons I Learned From My Mom

My Mom passed away a few years ago. The members of my family were invited to share any memories to honor my mother during the funeral service. Below are the 14 things I shared that I had learned from my Mom during her lifetime. I had planned on only doing 10, but a few more "snuck in" which I felt were too meaningful to leave out. Between Jesus and my Mom, I am grateful for the person I am today and who I will continue to grow and become in the future.

14. Keep your children's art work and enjoy it. Then return what you have collected over the years to them when they are adults, being sure to see the expression on their faces.

It was wonderful to see past creations from my own little hands that my Mom treasured enough to keep and then return to me in adulthood. I have enjoyed seeing my very first cartoon drawings again, a special sculpture I made in eighth grade, as well as the pastel drawing of the family dog.

13. Be sure to sit next to Uncle Jim when playing cards.

We had some relatives in the family who took card playing extremely seriously. My mother was not a card player and verbalized that to the others before the game started, to the delight of these relatives. However, my Uncle Jim proceeded to sit next to my mom and made sure to "feed" her the cards that would insure her winning almost every hand. This drove the "card sharks" crazy since they could not understand how such an amateur could do so well. We have kept this family secret until revealing it to you now.

12. When you see others in need, be sure to help, even if they don't ask.

My Mom taught us from a very early age to shovel the snow from our elderly neighbors' sidewalks, cut their grass or hedges as needed, check on them regularly, and visit them to see if they needed anything from the store. This behavior was MODELED by my Mom since I can remember; and, after watching for years, that behavior is well ingrained in my being. My brothers and I still help in these same ways today.

11. Teach everyone you know to make pierogies.

For those of you who don't know, pierogies are a Polish/Ukrainian food consisting of dough stuffed with various ingredients, but mostly, a potato and cheese filling. They are then boiled but can later be pan fried and eaten. It's a time-consuming process, but well worth the effort. When my Mom came to Atlanta to visit me some of my friends got together to learn how to make these calorie laden delights. We always hear how guys talk about getting closer during "male bonding," but that's nothing next to getting closer through "pierogie bonding."

10. When all the seats are taken in a public area (doctor's office waiting room, the bus, etc.) always give up your seat to your elders.

Even in my middle age, I still do this and probably will continue to even as I enter my golden years. It was MODELED and has been a part of me, and I expect will be forever. I remember when I was in the Army and stationed in Germany during the 1970's, giving up my seat to others on the trains we rode. When people realized that I was from the United States they were even more surprised at the gesture, since we were called "ugly Americans" back in those days.

9. Feed everyone who comes to your home.

When you visited my Mom's house, whether you were hungry or not, you would be fed. My friends would come over to visit and proceed to tell me if they ever fell on hard times, they knew they would never starve to death… they would just come by and see my Mom.

8. Red hair is awesome.

Blondes have more fun, but your kids can find you anywhere, anytime in a crowd when your mom has red hair. Other parents may have had those little "wrist leashes" to keep their children from becoming lost; but we had the "red hair alert" tracking system. GPS... eat your heart out!

7.   Never allow your sons to carry you up the stairs after breaking your ankle, especially if one of them is a comedian.

My Mom had broken her ankle and had a cast the length of her leg, which made it impossible for her to maneuver on the stairwell at her house. My brothers "helped" by making a little seat by joining hands and having my mom sit while they carried her up the steps. Of course, my brother Gary would make a joke about half-way up the stairs; and, my other brother, Frank, would start laughing uncontrollably and not be able to take another step. You would hear my Mom amid the fracas repeating over and over, "Don't you dare drop me!" Just for the record, they never did.

6.   When the fire siren goes off, grab the family dog and get out of the way.

My entire family were volunteer firefighters for our community and when the siren went off, they were all rushing out the door. Addendum: If the siren sounds at mealtime be assured that they will return at some point to finish the meal. Proviso: During night hours, the family dog is on this own.

5.   Always insist that there be a way to disarm the fire bells if they short out after a fire call.

Before the technology we now have was available, volunteer firefighters were alerted by the siren and a set of bells located within their homes. Please note, these were a very loud set of annoying bells. One day they went off, everyone left except for my Mom and I, and the bells continued to ring for two hours. I took the bell part off, but the clappers kept tapping and were still amazingly loud. We finally threw a pillow over the annoying thing and did our best to ignore it. When my brothers returned, we insisted that they find a way to shut them off in the event of this happening again. A switch was installed which we were all grateful, especially the dog.

4.   When you notice the mop strings disappearing from the mop stored on the porch it can mean only one thing, you now have an enterprising squirrel visiting you.

I remember my Mom noticing each time she mopped the kitchen floor that there were less mop strings available in order to clean. She began watching the porch and found that a squirrel was chewing and taking the mop away piece by piece. She allowed him to continue in his ways, feeling that the squirrel needed the mop strings more for his nest than she needed them to do the floors. I am convinced that the squirrel ended up with a 9 room "mop mansion" somewhere in our neighborhood.

3.   Try to fix anything that is broken.

My Mom could fix a TV from the 1950's with a set of new electronic tubes from the hardware store and some shoe strings. When the upholstery was worn on the two living room chairs, she took them apart, figured out how they were made, and sewed her own new ones. When the drapes were faded, she went to the fabric store, purchased another color and pattern, and made new ones. After watching her do this over the years, I learned not to be afraid to try and fix anything that is broken. After all, if it's "already" broken, how much more damage could be done trying to fix it?

2.   Know that you are truly special when your two sons have married such great wives, you have 5 wonderful grandchildren, and your daughter's pet parrot calls you "grandma."

1.   Know that you will be deeply missed by those who have had the privilege of sharing a lifetime with you. You have made a difference in so many lives and I am grateful to God for giving me such a special mom.

I look forward to meeting up with you in heaven, Mom, and getting to know all the angels you taught how to make pierogies.

"Honor your father and your mother,
so that you may live long in the land the Lord your God is giving you."
- Exodus 20:12

Day 28

The Anatomically Correct Heart And The Valentine Heart– Looks Aren't Everything

Do you remember being in school in February and drawing about a bazillion of those Valentine hearts to use as decorations? I am sure there are less of you who have for educational purposes, or for your own adventuresome self-learning curiosity, studied the anatomically correct heart from a medical book. Is it me, or do they just vaguely have any similarity? Sure, there are the two rounded parts at the top of the Valentine, that, I suppose, could in my deepest imagination resemble the two atriums of the human heart. Then the pointed bottom portion could be the apex of the ventricles, perhaps. Was the person who invented the Valentine heart even remotely looking at a "real" heart when he/she came up with the concept design?

To me the real human heart looks more like route 285 (the perimeter interstate circling the city of Atlanta, Georgia), or is it that route 285 looks like a chicken gizzard? Obviously, I can't remember and will need to check that out the next time I am having gizzards for dinner, a map of Atlanta available nearby, as well as a medical text. See there are unique learning opportunities even while having dinner. I like to call them "homeschool" moments, which are not unlike the old "Kodak" moments, only without pictures. But I digress from our comparison of the Valentine heart and the human heart.

I suppose, for me, the visual appearance of the human heart and the Valentine heart are very different, but the physiological functioning of the human heart needs to become the essence of the symbolism of the Valentine heart. Confused? I was also, so allow me to expand further.

The main purpose of the heart is to take the red blood cells and propel them throughout the body after they have gone to the lungs, their location of transformation. When a red blood cell comes into the heart, after its journey through the body, it is depleted of oxygen and is full of carbon dioxide, which is basically the icky waste from the other organs of the body. I like to picture the red blood cell as more of a "blue hued" blood cell with a frown on its face. It is tired, drained and exhausted in having to carry the burden of its journey back to the heart. There it comes into the atrium, the very entrance and welcoming center of this place of hope to come. Next, it travels to the most wonderful place of transformation itself, the place where it can release the burden that it carries. The lungs take that heavy load and replace it with new oxygen which the rest of the body MUST HAVE. Life cannot continue for the body without oxygen, nor without the lungs to make the exchange of vital gases (those of you with a junior high sense of humor, I hear you snickering), nor without the tiny red blood cell carrying it and especially not without a strong heart to interact between them all. What a wonder the heart truly is!

If we take the anatomical heart's purpose and place it within the symbolic Valentine, perhaps we can see a parallel for our lives. Spiritual and emotional hearts that are strong and well cared for are necessary for the link between those who are exhausted and the lung, which is the giver of life sustaining oxygen. We all have contact with others and tasks everyday which can become draining, tiring and exhausting. Our hearts are so vital, since these burdens and individuals need to enter the atrium of our caring and be released to the place of transformation. This is where we give up each burden and receive that which is essential to life... for ourselves and others. The very breath of God can come so deeply into each of us and for those we come into contact. Therefore, our heart can send out restoration through our interactions with others and in each task we undertake.

Are we not, then, that link between God and others in every part of our life? And even the everyday life that drains and stresses us can be given over to God as well. Does that not make each of us... a heart? We are the vital link between the physiological heart and the symbolic Valentine heart that we see in loving God and others. Just remember this when you cannot find the right Valentine gift for someone you love. Just put a bow on yourself and say you are their "heartfelt" gift… because you truly are… to them and to God.

"May the words of my mouth and the meditation of my <u>heart</u> be pleasing in your sight, O Lord, my rock and my Redeemer."
- Psalm 19:14

Day 29

What Do You Do When You Are Out Of Ammunition?

An excerpt taken from the website - Voices of Battle,
Gettysburg National Military Park Virtual Tour:

Colonel Joshua Chamberlain and the 20th Maine Infantry

"The Confederate attacks came in waves, each more intense than the one before.
At the height of the fighting, a Confederate bullet struck Chamberlain on his left
thigh. Luckily the metal sword scabbard hanging at his side diverted the bullet,
leaving him with only a painful bruise. The colonel leapt to his feet and continued
to encourage his men, directing the defense of the rocky hillside. The relentless
Confederate assaults shredded Chamberlain's ranks and the situation looked grim
as ammunition began to run out. Soldiers ransacked the cartridge boxes of the
wounded and dead strewn on the hillside, but there was not enough to continue for
much longer and that meager supply soon ran out. Chamberlain had not only been
directing his men, but closely observing the southern attacks as well. Sensing
exhaustion among the Confederates who were also probably running out of
ammunition, he formulated a final plan to defend the 20th Maine's part of the
shrinking Union line. There was a brief lull in the fighting when the colonel called
all his officers quickly to a meeting and explained his proposal- the 20th Maine was
going to make a charge!

*I (Chamberlain) stepped to the colors. The men turned towards me. One word
was enough- 'BAYONETS!' It caught like fire and swept along the ranks. The men*

took it up with a shout, one could not say whether from the pit or the song of the morning sat, it was vain to order 'Forward!' No mortal could have heard it in the mighty hosanna that was winging the sky...

It was a great right wheel. Our left swung first, the advancing foe stopped, tried to make a stand amidst the trees and boulders, but the frenzied bayonets pressing through every space forced a constant settling to the rear...

At the first dash the commanding officer I happened to confront, coming on fiercely (with) sword in hand and big navy revolver (in) the other, fires one barrel almost in my face. But seeing the quick saber point at his throat, reverses arms, gives sword and pistol into my hands and yields himself prisoner. "Ranks were broken; some retired before us somewhat hastily; some threw their muskets to the ground-even loaded; sunk on their knees, threw up their hands calling out, 'We surrender.'"

I would hope that anyone reading this will not look at the sides that would be chosen in this illustration, but rather the choice made in the face of overwhelming odds. I believe there are times in each of our lives where we feel surrounded and there is no more ammunition; when the enemy (spiritually) is advancing, and the very outcome of the battle depends on you holding your ground; when you want to run, and no one would blame you, even if you surrendered. It gives me such inspiration in seeing what Joshua Chamberlain decided to do in such a crucial battle… to charge forward with no ammunition, but with a great deal of conviction, spirit, and heart!

I have been to the site of this battle many times in Gettysburg, Pennsylvania. I have sat upon Little Round Top and looked down from where Chamberlain and the 20th Maine fought so bravely. Interestingly, the area below that site is called Devil's Den. The symbolism of the spiritual fight we have as believers always impressed me each time I would visit Little Round Top. As Paul states in I Timothy 6:12: "Fight the good fight of the faith. Take hold of the eternal life to which you were called when you made your good confession in the presence of many witnesses."

Let us do the same as Joshua Chamberlain, and charge forward to "fight the good fight" through the challenges of life.

"I have fought the good fight. I have finished the race. I have kept the faith."
- Timothy 4:7

Day 30

Being A Legend In Your Own Mind

A few weekends ago, I thought it was about time to explore my new surroundings since moving into my new apartment. There is a nature trail located within my complex, which is right next to my workplace, and the properties of the two meet along this very trail. I discovered this fact during my hike and came across the climbing wall of our summer camp program, and a smaller adjacent climbing "thingy" as well. I do not know what to call this smaller climbing "thingy" because to me it looked like... a boat. With my incredible imagination, it appeared to be a small version of Noah's Ark and with that vision, I became... Noah. I climbed the ladder of my newfound "ark" and looked out toward the horizon to search for the animals that should be coming two by two to this sanctuary before the rains began. In reality, there were about a dozen squirrels staring at me, wondering who the real "nut" was in the woods that day. Of course, being Noah, I called to them and encouraged them to get on board before it was too late. All that I could see were twelve fuzzy tails running off into the distance. Apparently, squirrels have no imagination.

I climbed down from my ark and moved on further into the woods, coming to the end of the tree line, and there before me was a large field leading to... the castle in the distance. OK... in reality it was the school and church building where I was employed, but it was too late, because I had hence become Joan of Arc and this was Paris, France. The siege for the final stronghold of the British was before me and I was charging across the field with banner and sword in hand for victory. Now I know that Joan of Arc never did take Paris after trying in battle, and I chose that particular conflict for a reason. After all, it does not seem right to conquer one's place of employment. After all, I needed to have a job to return to on Monday, now didn't I?

Coming back to reality, it seemed like a good time to do a few laps around the track, since I was so close to it and I needed the exercise. Arriving there, I picked the center lane and began running and suddenly found myself becoming Florence Griffith Joyner (popularly known as "Flo Jo"). Flying like the wind with long thin legs moving more quickly, I ran as fast as I could. OK… actually I was jogging and breathing rather heavily after a few laps and even another runner had lapped me by that point and was going to do so again, shortly. I suppose in reality I was more like Florence Henderson in my running technique. "Flo Hen," as she is not known as, seemed fitting if she took up the sport of track and field. Now for those of you not recalling who Florence Henderson is let me refresh your memories. She was the Brady Bunch mom, Carol Brady, who also had done commercials for one of those denture tooth glues that hold your false teeth in place while eating such impossible foods like apples and corn on the cob. Yes, "Flo Hen" and I have much in common on the track circuit and with Chicken Little… or would that be Kentucky Fried Chicken? Well, you be the judge.

After my invigorating run, I went back to the woods and came into the shadows once again. The trees and path were so inviting that I remembered back to when I was in elementary school and our favorite show was Robin Hood. Now this was a rather "campy" version that came on each morning before school and everyone in my first-grade class tuned in. We would talk about that morning's episode and then go forth to reenact the plot in the woods just off from the playground. So… there I was strolling through Sherwood Forest and I was wearing green from head to toe, so it was obvious that I was, no other than, Robin Hood. OK… in reality it was a green pair of sweatpants and an Aaron Rogers Green Bay Packers jersey but, nonetheless, it certainly was green. How appropriate for Robin Hood if only the number "12" could be removed from that jersey. Which only leads one to conclude; would Robin Hood have been a very good quarterback? How similar are shooting arrows and throwing footballs?

By this time, I had returned to my apartment pondering all these characters that I had become that morning. I remembered the enlightening school campus meeting, that we had a few weeks before this jaunt in the woods, about heroes and it seemed that each of these persons whom I imagined being were my personal heroes in one

72

way or another. Funny how those individuals from my past came back to me in seeing various environments on my walk. I can't help but wonder which heroes our children will be imagining they are when they are adults? Perhaps a few will let me know when that time comes.

"Sanctify them by the truth; your word is truth."
- John 17:17

Day 31

A Parrot's Love

It was a very cold day for being early in May and rain had been sporadically falling throughout the morning. To say the least, it was not very pleasant out at all. Perhaps that is why our little group of "feathery friends" was in such a "fowl" mood.

I love parrots and volunteer with an organization called Earth Quest, a non-profit environmental teaching organization, dedicated to the education of the public as to their impact on the natural world. The concept for Earth Quest began in the spring of 1989 as an idea to educate the general public about wildlife through the presentation of live animals in an entertaining format. The area of the organization which I work with is Parrots Without People, who sponsor the exhibit, Rescue Island, at the Georgia Renaissance Festival in Fairburn, Georgia.

We have an open-air aviary which provides a beautiful garden for approximately 20 or so parrots of various sizes and species. I knew it was going to be a "long" day when Petey, a Lesser Sulfur Crested Cockatoo and our most friendly parrot, began dive bombing people who came into the exhibit. After tiring of that, he then would fly to the ground, refusing to "step up" on command. His new past-time was finding guests who were wearing sandals and proceeding to attempt to bite exposed toes. A few children ran to the exit to escape Petey's attacks. It was not long before Petey was given a time out... yes, that is what you do with naughty parrots. We even have a time-out room, which works well since parrots are very social creatures and would rather not "miss out on the action."

With Petey removed from the aviary, I went on to visit another of my favorite parrots, Monkey. Monkey has been given that name because he is very capable of screaming like a monkey and does so very loudly. I have stood next to him and could not hear out of the ear facing his direction for many minutes after one of his screaming sessions. Monkey is a Malaccan Cockatoo, a very large and strikingly beautiful white and coral colored bird.

At first, I was afraid of going near Monkey, but, in time, I found that he enjoyed being cuddled and I would come beside him and place my hand around his back, and he would snuggle his head against me very sweetly. The other enjoyable trait of Monkey is that he loves to sing. He and I will do scales together and small "parrot operas" which also can become very loud. We usually have a crowd come to listen and then he shows off further with his dancing talents. To say the least, Monkey is one very animated and fun parrot!!!

But… this day was cold and rainy, and although Monkey was glad to see me, he was not quite himself. We were singing together when suddenly he reached over and bit me… very hard! I was shocked and stepped away from him. Rolling up my sleeve I noted the damage he inflicted and decided he needed to calm down, so I walked away to allow him a chance to settle. Later I went back, and once again during our duet, without warning, he took another strike at me with that large beak. I walked away again and the people who were watching me asked… "Does it hurt?" When I lifted my sleeve and showed them the huge bruise that was present, they gasped.

I have shared this story with many people since that weekend and have shown my "birdie battle wounds" as well. Most ask why I work with these creatures that do such harm. A few others have said that they would show that bird "a thing or two." I have allowed that question and comment to become a point to think about more fully. It has even become a part of my time of meditation and prayer with the Lord. I have asked myself… why do I continue to work with parrots, knowing that they will bite? Why do I own my African Gray Parrot, Galileo, when she, like Monkey, also bites, makes messes, tears up magazines when I am out, throws bird toys at the dog, and has done some damage to my furniture? Why put up with this behavior?

75

And then came to the same question regarding God. Why does the Lord put up with my behavior? Why would Jesus die for me knowing that there are days that I treat Him badly, say awful things to Him and others, make messes of my life, tear up the gifts that He gives so generously, throw insensitivity at others, and damage so much around me????

Why? Because He loves me… unconditionally… through all that I am, and all that I do.

On a much smaller level, I have those priceless moments where I share a special bond of love with these parrots… and I would not trade any of it away. That means that I am also willing to be bitten at times, and although it hurts, and leaves bruises, I still choose to care. In this symbolism of connection with one of God's creation, I understand just a little bit more of how much God loves me.

"So, do not be afraid; you are worth more than many sparrows (or in this instance… parrots)."
- Luke 12:6

Day 32

"Do You Hear What I Hear?"

I remember as a child learning to pray. Well, that is not exactly true. What I believe I was learning was how to "say" prayers. Now, you need to remember that I was raised Catholic, and we had some standard prayers that were "required" to be memorized and recited... and recited... and recited... and... and... and... you get the idea. Now, I believe there is a time for everything... even memorizing prayers and Scripture. So, please note, I am not advising the proverbial throwing of the baby out with the bath water.

In the learning of how to say these prayers, some of the words made little or no sense to me. What made it more interesting for me, in later years when my vocabulary and pronunciation had become more skilled, was that some of the words I had been saying as a child were entirely different than what the actual written words were in the prayer itself. My confusion in those early years was clarified as time went on, and I saw the error of my youthful naivety.

For example, the familiar prayer "Our Father" appears simple enough to say, don't you think? But as a child, I could never understand the very beginning of it: "Our Father, who art in Heaven, Hollywood be thy name." If I ever had to list the names for God, I imagine a part of the list back then would have included: Wonderful, Counselor, Prince of Peace, and, of course, Hollywood.

Or the prayer that was said, within my religious background, in which Elizabeth is so excited to see Mary that she exclaims: "Hail Mary, full of grapes!" Later I found the word was actually "grace," not grapes. I had wondered about Mary for a long time and this obsession with eating grapes. I concluded, for a time, that since she was with child, it was an equivalent of those cravings for things like pickles and ice cream. However, obviously at that time, only grapes were available, and, being the resourceful gal that she was... made do with what she had. Good ole' Mary, no wonder the angel came to her! Should I even go on to tell you that in this same prayer is another line that states: "Blessed are you amongst women." Not being a King James scholar as a child, you can imagine the very depths of my confusion when what I heard was: "a monk's woman." I was sure that the nuns had taught us that monks did not marry, but who was I to argue with a prayer. Then, you can really imagine my relief and great embarrassment on the day that enlightenment came to me, and the years of clouded understanding were dispersed. Oh, Kyrie eleison! (Translation from Latin: Oh, Lord have mercy!)

Why am I taking all of you along this stroll down memory lane? Simply to make the profound point that has become more poignant lately in the light of so many difficult issues and circumstances that surround all of us each day more tightly. There is a difference between saying prayers and praying. Talking "at" God is not the same as talking "with" God. It is the difference between something that we have heard before and are perhaps repeating without the depth of understanding or meaning. Or perhaps repeating that which has become habit, and not digging deeper into ourselves to do more and talk to Him from our hearts and minds. Taking the risk to tell Him about circumstances that make absolutely no sense, overwhelm us totally, or perhaps lead us to shut down completely can become the deepest time of prayer. To pray only that which is "politically" correct, even in Christian circles, may not be what our hearts truly need to tell God. And, if these thoughts and feelings are inside us already, somehow, I think that they will not be a devastating shock to our very Creator.

I wish to leave you with the blessing said before a meal by Sister Mary Clarence in the movie, "Sister Act." Is it the effort of heartfelt prayer, or the saying of a prayer? You make the call!

"Bless us, oh Lord, for these thy gifts which we are about to receive... and yea though I walk through the valley of the shadow of no food, I will fear no hunger. We want you to give us this day our daily bread... and to the republic for which it stands. And by the power invested in me, I now pronounce us ready to eat. Amen."

**"And when you pray, do not keep on babbling like pagans,
for they think they will be heard because of their many words."**

- Matthew 6:7

Day 33

How My Presence Relates To Your Presence While We Are In God's Presence

I remember in the Army while attending morning formation each squad leader would give "report," which was the status of those who were present or absent at that time. Normally you would hear, "all present and accounted for," since this was the morning roll call and you better have a good reason why you were not there physically. Since it was always so early in the morning most of us were present physically, but I'm not so sure we were mentally. This led me to wondering what is the exact, official definition of the word "presence?" Let me illuminate from our good friend, Webster's dictionary as it states: "the state of quality of being in a certain place; attendance, or the opposite of absence. Simply then, our presence in any one place means that we are there. But, I contend, that the truth is that, on some level, this is a fallacy. Let me explain further.

This morning, I woke up and stumbled to the bathroom and there, before me, in the mirror was this "person." She looked like me, but let's just say if you remember your Greek mythology, we could accurately refer to the person in the mirror as Medusa. In any case, I would confirm to you that my presence was there before the mirror, the actual state of being in that certain place; however, the quality of being in that place is another matter entirely. If someone would have ventured to ask me a question on any depth of thought, my inner Medusa would have responded with a vacant look and taken things further by turning the questioner into stone. As a word to the wise is sufficient, do not ask questions early in the morning of anyone with an inner Medusa.

The quality of being, or lack thereof, can also be observed in those who are involved deeply with the technological revolution. My physical presence can be seen in front of screens: television screens, computer screens, and on occasion in front of window screens; but my inner presence is in some faraway place often referred to as "la-la land." Others refer to it as "concentrating," but no matter what the name, the person is still inwardly and affectionately "out to lunch." I know many who have confided that they have observed this lack of presence quite often in their children! Hard to imagine, right? Think of how you feel when others are not even aware of you trying to get their attention. Or you receive a vague noise or an "ok", but you know they never heard what you said. Of course, you need to look in the mirror and be honest about how many times you do the same. Therefore, it must be concluded that anyone can be a "screenager" no matter what age they happen to be.

So, my presence does affect your presence, and your presence does the same to me. Perhaps with this awareness we will be able to unite both our physical and inner presence together in order to connect with those around us more fully. I think it is a novel idea!

But let's not forget the most important aspect of God's Presence. I am grateful to know that when I am praying, God's presence is there; fully and completely. I was trying to imagine those times when I am in distress, pouring out my heart to God within the depths of my soul, and as I finish, totally exhausted and then to hear: "Eh? Sorry, were you talking to me? Do you mind repeating that again please?" Of course, I have never heard those phrases from God… ever. He may not answer as I would have liked or perhaps said "wait" or even "no," but I am sure that He did hear me.

Thank you, Lord, that you do not reside in "la-la land!" Help us to change our address from that place in the very near future so we can connect fully with those around us.

Then Jesus looked up and said, "Father, I thank you that you have heard me. I know that you always hear me, but I said this for the benefit of the people standing here that they may believe that you sent me."
- John 11:41,42

81

Day 34

God And The WWE - World Wrestling Entertainment

Disclaimer: I am not a theologian and I do not play one on TV. Any resemblance between this writer and a theologian living or dead is purely coincidental. This writer is merely someone on this side of eternity taking each step as it comes and now shares one of those steps with you. Hopefully you will not trip while stepping out with her.

My Bible gives a summary statement before detailing the information that follows. The summary statement I wish to refer to reads: Jacob Wrestles With God. ...and Genesis 32:22-32 tells the "details at eleven" portion of the Scripture. My mind's eye illustrates this story in a most powerful and as always unique way. It is nighttime, and Jacob is alone when a "Man" begins wrestling with him until daybreak. And you thought those cage matches on the WWF and WWE were tough. Ha! They are mere child's play next to Jacob's all-nighter!!! Think about wrestling ALL NIGHT LONG with a very formidable entity -God! And it seems God initiated the match as verse 24 states: "So Jacob was left alone, and a Man wrestled with him till daybreak." Also, I find it interesting that God did not choose another sport instead of wrestling. After all God did not show up that night and begin a lacrosse team with Jacob, nor did he place him on a long lonely marathon. It was not a team sport where everyone was involved, nor was it a singular sport in solitude.

My direct experience with the sport of wrestling was in high school when I played on the basketball team for 4 years, and we often had to use the auxiliary gym for practice. Can you guess who used that gym for practice before we did? Yes, the wrestlers. Now the auxiliary gym did not have any windows nor the best ventilation, and when we first stepped through the doorway, I can remember nearly being knocked back out of the room by the smell alone. Wrestling is a very demanding and odiferous sport. It takes strength, endurance, fortitude, aptitude, strategy, quickness, and a great deodorant. I learned that wrestling is not for the faint of heart, body, soul...or nose for that matter.

All of us wrestle with our own personal struggles every day. Each of these struggles causes me to ponder so much about life and purpose and God and an endless array of subjects. I have never been one to latch onto pat answers since they are of little assistance or comfort to my mind and heart. In addition, I seem to find more and more questions instead of answers (not unlike the movie Yentl). So, what's a finite person to do??? I think God has shown up with a new sport to experience and it is not an easy one. Often it leaves me exhausted on several levels, and sometimes it just plain smells bad; but it is an intimate endurance of strength and perseverance with Him alone. It does not matter about the winner; it is about the experience of wrestling these issues together WITH Him. Allow me to state for the record... John Cena has nothing on me!!!

And, ultimately, I think I have discovered my WWE alias – Karen Lemon, The Masked Fruit!

"For our struggle is not against flesh and blood, but against the rulers, against the authorities, against the powers of this dark world and against the spiritual forces of evil in the heavenly realms."
- Ephesians 6:12

Day 35

Big Girls Don't Cry... Or Should They?

When my mother was with child, after having two sons, my parents were sure that this third child would also be a boy. They even went so far as to naming this child Sam. And then I came along and turned out to be, of all things (surprise, surprise) a girl! Although my official, legal name is Karen, the name that was used in referring to me was, you guessed it, Sam! Now I'm not sure if this beginning was a prelude to perhaps a part of my personality, but I learned how to tough it out through many things in my young life. For example, whether I wanted to or not, I learned to play baseball. My two brothers figured out that it was more proficient to play baseball with 3 players, rather than 2; therefore, I was recruited at the age of 5, to be the outfielder on this makeshift baseball team. Let me also note that we played with a regulation "hardball" baseball and that I was expected to make a play on the ball to the best of my young ability. So, if a fly ball was hit my way, I was taught how to get under it and attempt to catch it. Attempt is the operative word, because depth perception and coordination are a challenge at 5 years of age and more often than not, I would get beaned in the head. Consequently, I also began to cry because getting whopped with a hardball really did hurt... a lot. However, I was rebuked each time to toughen up and told to get back in the game. Crying held up the progression of the game and there was no time for such weakness. On the practical side as well, obviously, I had a hard-enough time catching the ball with clear vision, but with tears in my eyes... perhaps I may get seriously hurt and there goes the team's outfielder, heaven forbid! So, as expected, after a time, I took the baseball to the head without a single tear, even though it hurt like the dickens. As time marched further on and years drifted by, this lesson had a very deep impact on me... I basically stopped crying anytime I was hurt, whether the wound was physical or emotional. I had embodied, as the song states, "Big Girls Don't Cry."

Fast-forward to the present time... a time in which many stressors are suddenly surrounding me in almost every area of my life. Some of these situations are touching me in the deepest ways and are finally carving a chink in my emotional armor. To say the least, I have not appreciated it, have been fighting it, and when finally finding myself in tears, am responding with a great deal of anger for being so weak. For so many years I have thought of crying as basically a waste of time, energy, and emotions. I should just be able to shake off the pain, like I did playing baseball, and get back in the game. It has not been easy to do, if not in some ways impossible. This was especially true when my mother passed away and then Kitty, my best friend from childhood, followed a few months later. I still miss them so very much even today.

In a recent sermon at a local church, the special speaker for the day, referred to a gift he had received which definitely got my attention... a Jesus Action Figure. Recently I came across one of these referred to "action figures" at the mall and purchased one. This Jesus Action Figure comes with "poseable arms and gliding action," as it boasts on the packaging. The speaker referred to how, when reading Bible stories, we think of Jesus as just that... gliding about from one place to another with his hands extended, palms up, looking cool and detached... much like a Hollywood celebrity. Yet, that is not what one Biblical story tells us. When Lazarus died (John 11:1-44), Jesus went to Bethany with the knowledge that He was going to raise Lazarus from the dead. Now, Jesus could have arrived and said to Martha, Mary and all the others who were crying and wailing, "Lazarus will be fine. Everything will be fine because I am going to resurrect Lazarus from the dead. Now stop the emotional upheaval, shake off the pain and get back in the game. Quit being such a bunch of emotional weaklings." But, rather, as Scripture tells us... "Jesus wept." (John 11:35).

That sermon has made a major impact on me and I have reviewed it repeatedly, realizing that Jesus cared enough, felt enough, loved enough, hurt enough... to actually shed tears. Although that was then, and this is now, Jesus is the same yesterday, today and forever. I've pondered how much He cares in this present time and space about my new-found tears in the same way. If the Creator of the universe can cry, then it must be acceptable for a "big girl" like me to do so as well.

Now for my part, I just must share, I am in the process of giving up my Karen Action Figure.

How about you?

"You number and record my wanderings; put my tears into your bottle – are they not in your book?
- Psalm 56:8

Day 36

All You Need Is …

On my annual adventure towards Valentine's Day, I have found so many songs telling me of love. What it is, where it is, how it is, why it is, when it is, and, as mentioned above, that it is all I need. Love sounded like it was pretty important; after all, the word was everywhere. As a kid, I remember hearing the Beatles sing that "All you need is love," and then they broke up. The most popular singing group of the time disbanded and went their separate ways, causing many of us to ask, "Where's the love, man?" If this was the example of what I "needed," well, something seemed terribly wrong.

It was later that I heard another melody telling me, "Love is a many-splendored thing." A many-splendored thing? Love had now become "a thing," which kept me wondering, what exactly did it look like? Would I know if I saw it? And if I did see it… well then what do I do with it? It reminded me of my dog, Tiger, which I owned as a kid. Tiger "loved" to chase rabbits through the backyard. I ran through the neighbors' backyards… for blocks… while I chased after him and the frightened rabbit. Then one day it happened! The rabbit never saw the fence between the Fennel's and Wheeler's backyards and was knocked silly… totally stunned and just stood there unable to move. The bunny's bell had been rung! And Tiger stopped, just as stunned without even running into the fence, and just stared at the dazed rabbit. Tiger had finally caught what he chased after all his life and now that it was before him and available, he didn't have a clue what to do with it. Sound familiar, perhaps? So, for illustration purposes only, a dazed bunny and a chasing dog, like love, are many splendored-things. This I can partially attest to because I have seen people who have said they have "fallen in love" and they appear dazed and confused, just like a glassy eyed rabbit running into a fence at full speed.

So, what is this "falling in love" all about? Is it an eternal abyss that one "falls" into? Something that you cannot help because there you were walking along, minding your own business, and suddenly… you "fell" in love? Love must be very sneaky, because no one even knows what happened until it's too late and they have fallen in it. Did you know that another song claims, "Love hurts?" Well, one would expect so, if one were falling into an abyss, wouldn't one? Obviously, there is a bottom to that abyss since when you hit it, as the song so clearly states… love hurts. In my opinion, love is beginning to sound a bit like a group of jagged rocks just waiting for me to fall on them from a rather great height. Ouchy!

Another song claims that "love stinks." If we return to the falling part as talked about in the prior paragraph, then love must be something you fall into, and, I daresay, it does not seem like something pleasant if it "stinks". Maybe it is more like a puddle of something vile, and, again, you cannot help but take a fall into it. Might I suggest obtaining one of those little devices that calls the ambulance after you yell into it, "I've fallen, and I can't get up!" Be sure to mention that the Hazmat Team should also be summoned to the scene. It appears love is a messy business that clumsy, helpless people are attracted to against their will.

Then I found something that changed all those former concepts of love, even as they were being sung and shouted at me by so many different voices. It states: Love is patient, love is kind. It does not envy, it does not boast, it is not proud. It is not rude, it is not self-seeking, it is not easily angered, and it keeps no record of wrongs. Love does not delight in evil but rejoices with the truth. It always protects, always trusts, always hopes, and always perseveres. Love never fails. I Corinthians 13:4-8.

Perhaps, love is more than can possibly be imagined! Let's hope so, shall we?

"And now these three remain: faith, hope and love.
But the greatest of these is love."
- I Corinthians 13:13

Day 37

Happy "Holidays???" – Bah Humbug

I have been looking over the past year and reviewing the various "special days" that come along from month to month. I have been greeted with the following, beginning in January: Happy New Year, Happy Birthday, Happy Valentine's Day, Happy President's Day, Happy St. Patrick's Day, Happy Easter, have a nice Memorial Day, Happy Fourth of July, Happy Labor Day, Happy Halloween, Happy Thanksgiving, and now… Happy Holiday. Happy Holiday? What does that mean exactly?

Why is it that for all the other holidays throughout the year people call them by their exact name? No one once wished me a "Happy Holiday" in place of the name of the particular days cited in the prior paragraph. I keep hearing that some people don't want to say Merry Christmas because someone might be offended. I keep trying to understand this concept.

I remember working at a private school in Pittsburgh and one of the teachers there was Jewish. The first year I forgot and wished Nan a Merry Christmas. She smiled and said, "Have a Happy Hanukkah;" and it was then that I realized I had forgotten she was Jewish, but all was well. She was not offended but reminded me of her faith. The next year I remembered and wished her a Happy Hanukkah, and she wished me a Merry Christmas. I felt more of a bond with Nan in doing so because we were recognizing our differing beliefs in God. It was Nan who showed me the graciousness of respecting and caring for each other in a complete way, and isn't that showing others that "love is patient, love is kind?" Because of her example, Nan will always hold a special place in my memories and heart. To me just wishing each other a Happy Holiday seems to negate who we really are and what we deeply believe. I find that rather ironic in a society that wants us to all understand and respect one another, don't you?

Perhaps some of you know who Ben Stein was. Most remember him as the actor who was often cast as a teacher with a monotone voice and expressionless face in movies and television. He was also a presidential speech writer and occasionally offered commentaries for the CBS Sunday News program. The item below is based on one such commentary entitled, "Confessions for the Holidays" and was delivered by Mr. Stein during that program on December 18, 2005. I think you will find it to be most interesting regarding those who insist on limiting all of us to the term "Happy Holidays."

"Next confession: I am a Jew, and every single one of my ancestors was Jewish. And it does not bother me even a little bit when people call those beautiful lit up, bejeweled trees Christmas trees. I don't feel threatened. I don't feel discriminated against. That's what they are: Christmas trees. It doesn't bother me a bit when people say, 'Merry Christmas' to me. I don't think they are slighting me or getting ready to put me in a ghetto. In fact, I kind of like it. It shows that we are all brothers and sisters celebrating this happy time of year. It doesn't bother me at all that there is a manger scene on display at a key intersection near my beach house in Malibu. If people want a creche, it's just fine with me as is the Menorah a few hundred yards away.

I don't like getting pushed around for being a Jew, and I don't think Christians like getting pushed around for being Christians. I think people who believe in God are sick and tired of getting pushed around, period. I have no idea where the concept came from that America is an explicitly atheist country. I can't find it in the Constitution, and I don't like it being shoved down my throat.

Or maybe I can put it another way: where did the idea come from that we should worship Nick and Jessica (Nick Lachey and Jessica Simpson - who are no longer a couple), and we aren't allowed to worship God as we understand Him?

I guess that's a sign that I'm getting old, too. But there are a lot of us who are wondering where Nick and Jessica came from and where the America we knew went to."

I suppose, like Ben Stein, there are still some of us who must be getting old also. I'm ok with that and, hopefully, so are you.

"And the king gave a great banquet,
Esther's banquet, for all his nobles and officials. He proclaimed a holiday
throughout the provinces and distributed gifts with royal liberality."
- Esther 2:18

Day 38

Simply Simple Spiritual Simplicity

Once upon a time, a long time ago; or perhaps it only seemed that way; life appeared to be much more... how shall I say... simplistic.

I remember when the most expensive worldly possession I owned was my Fender acoustic guitar which had a value of approximately $275. It went to Bible studies and small group worship gatherings where the only 6 chords I could play were converted into about 100 different songs. For those of you who remember the <u>Rejoice In Jesus Always</u> song book, you know exactly what I am referring to.

I remember a time when the suitcase with all my civilian clothes was lost for 3 months after the Army sent it to Fort Lee, Virginia while I was stationed in Fort Hamilton, New York... which I suppose are not all that far away from each other, except regarding a suitcase containing all you own. All the civilian clothes I wore during that time were donated to me by a fellow soldier who worked in the personnel office on the base. I must admit that I had the most well-worn, soft denim, light blue jean jacket that constantly evoked compliments from others. All the clothes he gave to me were old and worn, but so very comfortable that I really enjoyed wearing them. I had the "shabby chic" look well before it became popular and I was very grateful for his kind generosity.

I remember a time when I had no checking account, only a savings account. I did not carry any credit cards but traveled all over Germany and Europe. I did not carry a purse or a conventional wallet. I had received a small New Testament/Psalms Bible from the ministry where I had become a believer and in the front cover, I would place my military ID and the money that I had in my possession, which fit easily in that small space. That Bible doubled as my wallet, which I would open and read any time I was waiting or traveling, especially when riding on the trains overseas.

I remember a time when there were no computers, no internet, no iPods, no Walkmans, no BlackBerries (except for the ones that were edible and grew on vines in the woods), no cell phones, no Bluetooth (unless you didn't rinse off the original formula Crest toothpaste after brushing), no cable access, no broadband, and no remote controls.

I remember a time when I had no desire to watch TV, but would rather go back to the Army Chapel, that I worked at, after dinner in the mess hall, and spent time working with the Chapel Youth Group. I remember when I would walk through the woods, across meadows, and up hillsides, especially in Germany, for an entire day and enjoy God's beautiful creation, stopping to look at everything around me and drink it in so deeply. Times that I would stop, and sit, and read the Psalms from my little Bible while listening to the birds singing all around me. The times when I would stop and coax the horses in the fields to come to the fence, so I could pet them and rub their velvet noses. OK, I know that borders on being campy or corny, but it was how I felt in those days. Perhaps it was the faith of a little child and sadly, it changed over many years.

I remember a time when it was Christmas and all the choir members at the military chapel had traveled from the base to be with friends or relatives. The chaplain was disappointed that there would only be the playing of the organ without an organized group singing along on such a special holiday. I contacted some friends from another base and asked them to come and be the choir for Christmas morning, and so they arrived the night before. The only place I had for them to stay overnight was the balcony of the sanctuary, and all of us slept there surrounded by the stained-glass windows as the light of the morning crept in. All I could think of was how special it was to sleep in God's house on Christmas Eve and awaken there on Christmas morning.

I remember a time when I was a very new Christian believer and did not understand much more than I was a sinner, Jesus died for me, I asked Him to come into my heart, I knew that He had, I trusted Him with my life, He was changing my life daily, and I really wanted to know and to do His Will. Everything I did... I recognized that He was right there with me, and I talked to Him all the time. I would go jogging with Jesus (doesn't that sound like some church work-out class?) or play basketball with Him (He always seemed to win), or just sit and look at a sunset... the activity didn't matter. I just wanted His closeness and longed for His fellowship in the Word, in prayer, in meditation, in my everyday tasks... in everything.

At some point in life I believe we all come to a landmark year, whether we admit it or not, and look back over life, as most do in their middle ages, and feel something is missing. I began longing for that past intimacy and simplicity in my relationship with Jesus!!!! Even as I have written the above paragraphs, each memory stirs something deep within my heart. Each was such a special time with God and the underlying yearning was becoming a desperate need of something I had to have once again. Perhaps you have heard the saying: "If you're not close to Jesus, guess who moved?" But I would not say that I moved or that Jesus did... I still had a relationship with Him; but perhaps I discovered I was taking Him for granted. I do not know for sure, but I pray that I would once more be close to Him with that same simple spiritual intimacy that I once knew.

How simple have you been lately?

"So I say to you: Ask and it will be given to you; seek and you will find; knock and the door will be opened to you."
- Luke 11:9

Day 39

Police Officer Murphy (Or Should I Say)... Officer Mercy

Yes, I was in a hurry. It was about 10:20 at night, after evening services at my church, after a long day at work, and all I wanted to do was to get home. I was tired and the cars in the right lane on Old Milton Parkway were going slower than a herd of turtles. So, I was passing them... much too quickly and when I passed the two police cars on the side of the road, I knew that I was speeding and deserved to be stopped. I had already pulled over to the right turn lane even before the blue lights appeared and waited for the police car to come up behind me. Next were the extremely bright spot lights just like the television show COPS. This was the first time I had ever been pulled over by the police and I am sure I heard the theme from COPS playing as the police officer approached my car. "Bad boys, bad boys whatcha gonna do? Whatcha gonna do when they come for you?" I knew what I was going to do... I was gonna get a ticket with a great big fine and maybe a day at traffic court. Indeed, that's what I was gonna do!

First, I drive way too fast and I have always admitted it. I have even said to many people over the years that the day I get pulled over for speeding, I would have no excuses. Well, that day had finally come. Even before Officer Murphy approached my car, I had my license and registration in hand and the window down. I knew what to do, after all, I watched COPS every Saturday evening. Please follow along as my encounter with Officer Murphy went like this:

<u>Officer Murphy</u>: "Good evening, Ma'am."

<u>Me</u>: "Good evening, officer."

<u>Officer Murphy</u>: "We clocked you going 65 mph in a 45-mph speed zone."

<u>Me</u>: "I was doing at least 60 mph officer, so that sounds about right." (When I looked down at my speedometer, after seeing the two police cars and letting off the gas pedal, I was going 60, so 65 was most likely what I was going when they spotted me. It was all correct as far as I was concerned.)

<u>Officer Murphy</u>: "May I see your license and registration please?"

<u>Me</u>: (Having both in hand, I passed them to him.) "Would you like my insurance card also?"

<u>Officer Murphy</u>: "No, this is fine. I'll be back with you shortly." (He returned to his patrol car.)

<u>Me</u>: "Yes, Sir." (My thoughts at the time: Well, you know you drive too fast and that this day would come. Twenty miles over the speed limit. I wonder how much that will cost? I wonder how many points toward my license? I bet I'll be in court also. There goes a great deal of time and money... especially the money since I'm a rather frugal person. Well Lord, I deserve it. I know better and it's the day of reckoning regarding my driving. I know You are trying to tell me something, and that's the need to slow down, not only on the road, but on the road of life as well. If this is what it takes, and obviously it is, then this is what it takes.) Officer Murphy returns to my car.

<u>Officer Murphy</u>: "So where do you teach school?"

<u>Me</u>: (How does he know I work at a school? Duh, I've got the "Support Education" tag on the back of my car, Genius.) "Well, I'm not a teacher. I do work at a school... Perimeter Christian School." (What a wonderful Christian example this is turning out to be... NOT!) I'm the school manager and school nurse. (What does that have to do with speeding? Why is he asking this???)

<u>Officer Murphy</u>: (Handing back my license and registration.) "I'm not going to cite you for speeding?"

<u>Me</u>: (The look on my face was one of shock and disbelief. I wanted to say, "You have got to be kidding??? Twenty miles over the speed limit and I'm not getting a ticket? Are you crazy?" But what came out of my mouth was...) Thank you, officer. I do understand what you have done, and I greatly appreciate it." (At this point I also noticed my Bible sitting in the passenger seat. Could I have done any worse job of Christian witnessing???)

<u>Officer Murphy</u>: "My mother's a teacher and I appreciate those who are in education. But I am giving you a VERY STRONG WARNING. You have got to SLOW DOWN!

<u>Me</u>: "Yes, Sir. And I will do so. I was just coming home from church and was tired and needed to get home. (Karen... I can't believe you are talking about

96

CHURCH now on top of everything you have done. No more references to church, or anything Christian, OK? You've done enough damage to setting an example for your beliefs. Good grief, girl... just stop!!!!)

Officer Murphy: (nodding) "Just be sure you slow down and drive safely. Don't let me catch you speeding through here again."

Me: "Yes, officer... and thank you, again."

I proceeded home... without speeding and after turning off the engine I just sat there. The Holy Spirit spoke to me at that point: You broke the law and deserved to be punished with a huge fine, points on your license and traffic court. This police officer showed you "a great deal of mercy" in giving you a warning. I know you understand that. In the greater scheme of life and the larger magnitude from this situation, do you understand that you have broken God's law by sinning? Do you really understand that God cannot have sin in His Presence. And do you see by a practical example in life that Jesus showed you TOTAL MERCY before God by dying on the cross for every sin and violation you have done and will do in your life? Do you understand how much we (Father, Son and Holy Spirt) completely and totally love you?

Yes, Lord. You have brought it home in a most real and tangible way. Thanks for the "hands-on" lesson.

Also... a special thank you to Officer Murphy, who's name will from henceforth be known as "Officer Mercy."

"It (love) keeps no record of wrongs."
- I Corinthians 13:5

Day 40

Spiritual Risk

A few years ago, I was making the rounds at Office Depot and went by the discounted computer game section. These are usually games that have been on the market for a while and are not very popular any longer. They are also ones that have been discounted to a price that I can justify making the purchase. You can fully believe me when I tell you that you will never see me camping out in front of Best Buy in fair or foul (or even fowl) weather, waiting for the debut of the next version of Play Station or Game Boy... or Game Man or Woman, for that matter. With this introduction in mind, let me digress to the past for a moment.

As most of you know I spent time in the U.S. Army. Of course, this was way back in the ancient times of technology when we were marveling at the most high-tech game of the times called Pong. My Army salary consisted of a take home pay of $401 per month. Somehow, I could not justify purchasing the most modern video game of the time. The good news is that I was stationed with individuals who were equally poor, and we had to resort to another form of gaming called – board games. The favorite board game that my friends and I played was none other than... Risk.

If you are not familiar with the game of Risk allow me to explain that it is a challenge of strategy in which each player has an army and the object of the game is to win battles and take over countries across the world. The person who would deploy their troops well and had some favorable rolls of the dice, would eventually take over the world. This is not a very quick task as you can imagine, after all, it does involve world domination. Sometimes Risk would make Monopoly look like a 100-meter sprint as compared to an entire marathon. We would play Risk through an entire day, evening and into the wee hours of the morning as battles were fought with dice and little plastic pieces that came in various colors. Somehow being in the Army and playing Risk seemed to go hand in hand. I have very fond memories of those times and especially of those friends who bonded together over something as simple as a board game. Ah, times were rather simple back then.

Meanwhile back at Office Depot a familiar name caught my eye in all those computer games. Could it really be true? There on the cover of the CD was a cavalry troop charging with swords drawn and the name jumping right off the box... RISK!!! Now, I realize that this is probably not headline news to those of you who keep up with the latest computer games; but, for me, it was a revelation. As you can most likely guess, that game went right into the basket to be purchased.

Even though I had the game it was a couple of weeks before I found the time to put it in my computer and play. I suppose that made the anticipation of discovery even greater. For me this was a very impressive version of the board game since my little troopers were graphics of tiny people in uniforms. The uniform colors could be chosen and there was even the color pink. How about that? I know how "girly" that sounds but I was impressed.

Finally, I investigated the entire game, took on my opponents, fought valiantly... and lost. How disappointing. So, I thought my battle plans further and played again... and lost. It's hard to admit that I played an entire evening and through the night until 6:00 am. Yes, it was 6:00 am and I am shaking my head in disbelief even as I type this. However, I improved with each game and started to be one of the last armies to stay in the game, but I never won. I finally turned the computer off and thought that I would certainly be ready for the next round of battle when I had the time to play again.

I must admit that games of strategy greatly intrigue me, especially military ones. I like having to think through a course of action while my opponent does the same, and that each move requires me to spontaneously think through another approach to the situation. I am not sure why I enjoy these challenges because, as I have admitted in my prior paragraph, I am obviously not the best at winning such games. By the way, you need to be aware that I had never won in playing the board game version of Risk either.

A few days later, my time of going into battle came once again. This time I was careful not to spread my troops too thin, and I began to see more and more of the map being taken over by my army. It seemed too good to be true! I took over and conquered one army and then another, which meant I was also beating the computer this time around. It was down to the last army and my own fighting over the final country. Victory was mine!!!! I looked at the globe on the screen and, as it turned, there was nothing in all the countries but the color of my winning army. Pink never looked so good!

Now, my question to you is: what would you be feeling if you were in my shoes, or Army boots in this case?

I expected to feel such triumph in this victory, and I did, but for a very short period of time. Just a couple of minutes to be exact. For all the accomplishment in consideration of losing to the computer so many times, in never winning at the board game version with my friends, and in the knowledge, it is only a game… I had one single, solitary thought come to mind. It was about as unexpected as could be.

Before reading on, I challenge you to verbalize what you are thinking right now. What is the single, solitary thought in your mind if you had finally won this game and took over the entire world?

The only thought in my mind was from Matthew 16:26: "For what profit is it to a man (or woman) if he (or she) gains the whole world and loses his (her) own soul?" How very strange that God shows up and has something important to say even when playing a computer game.

So, what were you thinking?????

> **"When I was a child, I talked like a child, I thought like a child,**
> **I reasoned like a child.**
> **When I became a man, I put childish ways behind me."**
> **- I Corinthians 13:11**

Notes

Made in the USA
Columbia, SC
18 March 2019